The Jonathan Club Story

First Edition

Published in the United States of America by
Balcony Press 2005

Design by Scott Rivera

Printed in South Korea

No part of this book may be reproduced in any manner without written permission. For information address:

Balcony Press
512 E. Wilson, Suite 213
Glendale, California 91206

The Jonathan Club Story ©2005 Jonathan Club

Library of Congress Catalog Card Number: 2005922066

ISBN 1-890449-33-4

Endpaper Image: *Brother Jonathans*, hundreds of them, represent Yankee volunteers marching into Dixie at the beginning of the Civil War in this sheet music cover published by C.F. Morse in 1862.

The Jonathan Club Story

Nat B. Read

BALCONY PRESS

LOS ANGELES

Those who made this book possible

BOARD OF DIRECTORS 2003-2004

Brian J. Seery, President
John B. Hendricks, First Vice President
Douglas M. Laidlaw, Second Vice President
Christopher A. Higgins, Vice President
James J. Feder, Secretary
Michael E. Flynn, Treasurer
John J. Costello, Director
Patricia M. Griffith, Director
Mark C. Higgins, Director
Mathew M. Pendo, Director
Nat B. Read, Director
Thomas Brennan, Immediate Past President

BOARD OF DIRECTORS 2004-2005

Patricia M. Griffith, President
James J. Feder, First Vice President
Michael E. Flynn, Second Vice President
Mathew M. Pendo, Secretary
Mark C. Higgins, Treasurer
John J. Costello, Director
J. Peter Devereaux, Director
James E. Mahoney, Director
Christopher E. Maling, Director
Margaret C. Merrill, Director
Nat B. Read, Director
Brian J. Seery, Immediate Past President

Book Oversight Task Force

John B. Hendricks, Chair
John Holoman
Douglas M. Laidlaw
Michael Lindsey
David Meshulam
Mathew M. Pendo

Contents

Foreword   6

1. Beginnings   9
2. Pacific Electric Building   25
3. Sixth and Figueroa   43
4. Town Club Spaces   69
5. Depression   117
6. Jonathan Club at the Beach   125
7. War   137
8. Recent Times   145
9. Art   153
    Appendices   171
    References
    Index

FOREWORD

This book is written in a year of significant anniversaries for the Jonathan Club. The year 2005 marks the 110th anniversary of the Club's founding, the 100th anniversary of its move to the Pacific Electric Building, the 80th anniversary of its move to its present Town Club, the 75th anniversary of its presence on the Santa Monica Beach, the 70th anniversary of its reorganization from The Jonathan Club to Jonathan Club and the 70th anniversary of its purchase of the present Jonathan Beach Club.

The research path to this book offered many surprises. It turns out that the history of the Jonathan Club, told and retold for generations, was fundamentally wrong in many regards, beginning with its creation myths. Some of the most fascinating chapters of the Club's history had been beautified, sterilized or covered up in Club literature. The struggles for power that so changed the Club had been replaced with tales of one-dimensional cardboard heroes. Other interesting turns in its history had been long forgotten. Who remembered the Jonathan Country Club in Mexico? Or that The Jonathan Club, utterly broke, was sold on the courthouse steps?

To compile the Club's history I read every page of every Club magazine, beginning with its 1930 re-start. No copies of the original *The Jonathan* magazine published during World War I are still in Club archives. I read every page of every set of board minutes up to current years. I dogged the stacks of many libraries, scrolled through countless files of microfilm and microfiche, studied faded maps, consulted librarians and historians and sifted through every historic sheet I could find in the Club. I read every scrap in the collection of the papers of Henry Edwards Huntington and other early members, at the Huntington Library, for the years of their Jonathan Club involvement.

My journey began as nothing more than a pleasant diversion of sifting through Club history to satisfy my own curiosity. The thought of compiling the research into a book came much later. Two successive boards voted to give the book the backing of the Club.

Many who have been deeply involved in the Club over a number of years will be disappointed that their names are not mentioned in these pages. But, the book is intended as an album of the facilities of the Jonathan Club and a chronicle of its institutional life, not an encyclopedic compilation of the names involved.

For the Club's centennial in 1995, a book, *Jonathan – A Celebrated Club*, was compiled by Sally R. Guthrie, a former Jonathan Club magazine editor. That book was a fascinating and well-written memento prepared as a gift for the memorable 100th year event itself, and I am most grateful to her and to the Centennial Committee for their volume. That book drew primarily from past issues of *The Jonathan* magazine, without original research to confirm or dispel the stories on its pages, and its author cannot be blamed that so much of the magazine lore of former years turns out to be different from the accounts in the Club's publication.

I am most grateful to the boards of the Club who agreed on the need for an authoritative history of their institution, and I give special thanks to general manager Norm Rich and the Jonathan Club staff who were tremendously supportive throughout this project. Too much praise cannot be given to Robert Johnson, who held many positions in the management of the Club over the past few decades, and who served as interim manager on four different occasions. Bob Johnson appreciated the Club's history when few others did, preserving documents, collecting artifacts and establishing a Club museum. I must also salute Daniel Lewis and others on the staff of the Huntington Library for their invaluable encouragement and assistance.

This book is one writer's summary, by no means complete, and selective in what to include and what to edit out. I hope this work will inspire others to do further research and writing about this unique club. The detailed documentation of the sources for the facts and accounts on these pages will be left in the Club archives for future researchers, so that the Club history, so painstakingly discovered in this project, can be shared and built upon in the future.

Nat B. Read
Los Angeles
2005

Chapter 1
BEGINNINGS

1781 – City of Los Angeles settled   1821 – Mexican rule of Los Angeles replaces Spanish rule   1850 – California admitted to the U.S.; Los Angeles becomes an American city   1850 – Los Angeles population is 1,610   1860 – Los Angeles population is 4,385   1869 – First local railroad: Los Angeles – San Pedro   1870 – Los Angeles population is 5,728   1880 – Los Angeles population is 11,183   1880 – Los Angeles Athletic Club founded   1880 – University of Southern California founded   1882 – First telephone in Los Angeles

This popular postcard from the turn of the twentieth century showed the heart of that day's Downtown Los Angeles, South Spring Street. The two early Jonathan Club locations are on the left side of the street between First Street (where the trolley is entering the intersection) and Second Street farther away.

1894 WAS A LONG TIME AGO

The time of the Club's founding is an eternity away from present-day Los Angeles. There were no cars in this auto capital of the world. People moved about the city in horse-drawn carriages, on bicycles or by horse-drawn rail cars. Electric trolleys were being tried in Los Angeles just as The Jonathan Club came into existence. The new electric street lighting was turned off on moonlit nights. Firemen had to hitch up a team of horses before racing to a fire.

The population of Los Angeles was about 70,000…the size of Bellflower in 2000. There were about 13,000 voting Republicans in the city and about 11,000 Democrats.

Thirty years doesn't seem like a long time. Only 30 years before the Jonathan Club was founded, Los Angeles was a small dusty town, with fewer than 5,000 inhabitants, and the president was Abraham Lincoln. The streets of Los Angeles were unpaved, there was no bank or public school system and there were no telephones. Orange trees had yet to be planted here, and oil had not yet been discovered in Southern California. Such were the memories in 1894, of those few who had grown up here.

1882 — Electric lights installed in Downtown Los Angeles

1882 — Future Jonathan Club member Harrison Gray Otis buys Los Angeles Times

1885 — First paid firefighters in Los Angeles

1886 — Coin-operated motion picture machines in Los Angeles

1886 — Future Jonathan Club member Griffith J. Griffith donates 3,500 acres as the nation's largest urban park

1887 — California Club founded

1887 — Orange County carved from Los Angeles County

1890 — Los Angeles population: 50,395

1890 — Last major battle of U.S. troops vs. Indians, at Wounded Knee

1892 — First oil well in Los Angeles at 2nd St. and Glendale Blvd.

1894 — Thomas Edison's motion picture kinetoscope's first public showing

The building at 130 South Spring Street was home to the orginital Jonathan Club Republican organization in 1894 and was the home of the social Jonathan Club in 1895 before the club moved next door to 132 South Spring. In this photograph the building is decorated for a parade or other public spectacle.

The founding of the Club

The founding date of the Jonathan Club is so important to its members that it is literally set in stone at the entrance to its Town Club. In fact, it is set in stone twice, 12 feet apart. Yet the two dates are different!

This schizophrenia reflects the founding of a political group, in 1894, and its segue into a purely social group, in 1895. The Club today bases its anniversaries on the 1895 date.

The original Jonathan Club was organized on April 30, 1894, by a group of young Republicans who preferred each other's company to that of the hoi polloi, ordinary Republicans. They wanted a clubhouse where they could schmooze, booze and entertain unpolluted by the rank-and-file Republicans from the Republican Club, around the corner on First Street.

The youthful exuberance of the new club was ridiculed by some. A letter to the *Los Angeles Herald* said, "If the 'war cry' of the new Republican club is a fair criterion on which to base an estimate of the intelligence and wisdom of that club, then it must be of a very low order, in fact bordering on the idiotic. …The upcoming campaign (election of 1894) is one in which uniforms, torchlights and wah-ho-wah songs will produce little effect. …all this tomfoolery of war cries and spectacular demonstrations will fall flat. …Political clubs should be made up of thinking men instead of 'jolly sports'."

The Jonathan Club was formed at the Hollenbeck Hotel the evening of April 26, 1894. According to the *Los Angeles Express* it was "a Republican club with social features," patterned after the Dirigo Club of San Francisco. It was proposed that this club "not … in any way conflict with other clubs," a possible reference to the Los Angeles Republican Club being organized at the same time and which planned to welcome all Republicans to its ranks. Committees were appointed for permanent organization, constitution and by-laws, membership, rooms, and a name for the club, and plans were made to reassemble to "elect officers and perfect the organization" on April 30.

The original club members hosted state and local political candidates, took trains to political rallies in nearby cities such as Pasadena, and gathered on weekends for entertainment socials. The club members boasted a band of their own, and they took their band to rallies and marched with Japanese lanterns on short poles which rested across their shoulders. They wore Jonathan Club badges and sailor hats with "Jonathan" on the caps' bands of ribbon and some members carried oversized letters spelling out the club name. And they whooped their war cry: "Wah-hoo-wah, wah-hoo-wah, Jonathan, Jonathan, wah-hoo-wah!"

Governor Henry Markham was present on May 19th for the official opening of the Club's quarters at 130 South Spring. The Club was limited to 100 members, sixty of whom had signed up by the time of the formal opening. By July, the Club expanded by renting additional rooms at the same address, and by August it had installed billiard tables.

Was the Club founded to support William McKinley?

In their later years, early members of The Jonathan Club said that the Club had been founded in 1894 to support the presidential candidacy of William McKinley. But McKinley was not nominated for the office until the Spring of 1896, half a year after the club dropped its Republican ties and became strictly non-partisan. In their senior years, founding members said that they had segued to a social club after the McKinley election, because by then they had bonded, had liquor left over and wanted to go on meeting together. Of course, that can't be true since McKinley was elected in 1896 and they had shifted to a social club in 1895. What they probably remembered is shifting to a social club after the election...but the election of 1894, not 1896. Right rationale; wrong election!

Why did the Club members put so much public energy behind state and local Republican candidates with no public drum-beating for their supposed central subject? Why would they disable the political purpose of their club at the very time they could help McKinley the most?

But if it's so unlikely that McKinley prompted the founding of the original Jonathan Club, why did some of its early members have such a recollection in their elder years?

The answer may lie in the fact that McKinley became an American martyr after his assassination, in 1901, in much the same way that John F. Kennedy became a national icon after his assassination, in 1963. Jonathan Club members had undoubtedly worked with one another to elect McKinley, and many of the members no doubt met President McKinley when he visited Los Angeles, in 1900. It is not surprising, then, that their chronology got mixed up many years later.

It is likely that the errant connection with McKinley was started by John Bushnell, an original board member of the 1895 Club and the early historian of the Club. In his later years Bushnell consistently tied the 1894 Club founding to McKinley and he consistently placed the social club's 1895 charter *after* the 1896 McKinley election. The first known mention of The Jonathan Club/McKinley hypothesis came in a *Los Angeles Times* account of the death of the (social) Club's first president, George Alexander, on Aug. 21, 1913, 19 years after the original organization's founding. It is perhaps significant that the article mentions John Bushnell, who may have been the newspaper's source.

How did The Jonathan Club get its name?

The founders of the 1894 Republican organization named themselves The Jonathan Club. One of the original directors, Ed Tufts, suggested the name. When the members chartered themselves as a social club in 1895, they seriously considered the name Los Angeles Club but ended up keeping the name Jonathan Club.

So, who was Jonathan?

The United States of America has known three personifications in its two-plus centuries. Prior to the Revolutionary War the Colonists were caricatured by Yankee Doodle. Between the Revolutionary War and the Civil War, Americans were symbolized by Brother Jonathan. After the Civil War, the icon of Uncle Sam came to signify the U.S.A..

Southern California Republicans of the late 19th century had grown up with the Brother Jonathan symbol of America. He was the patriotic national character of their youth, and of their parents' and grandparents' times.

Brother Jonathan, the counterpart to Britain's John Bull, was invented to characterize the brash, new experiment in democracy. He was a rural New England commoner, like Yankee Doodle before him. Brother Jonathan had the audacity to believe himself as valued a citizen as the educated aristocrat and this infant nation was naive enough to count their two votes with the same weight.

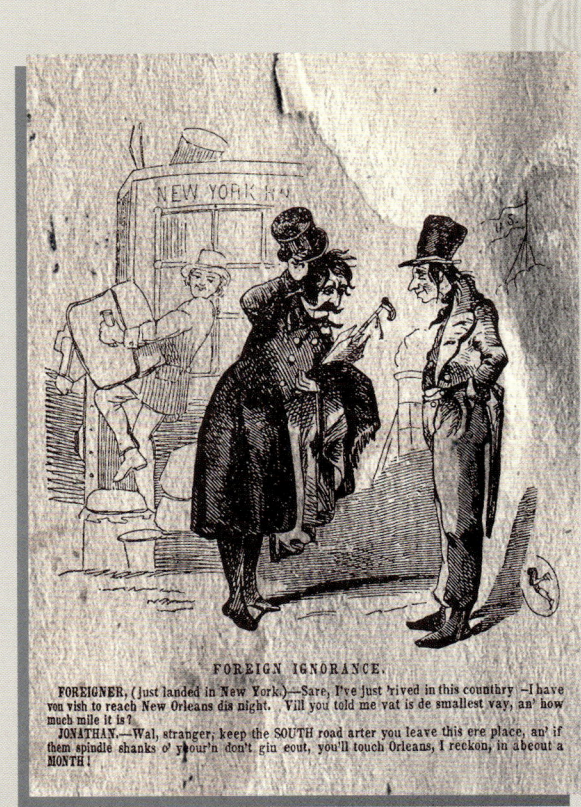

Brother Jonathan was, in fact, counterpoint to the aristocrat. All Western societies before his had sported elite classes, and although there was a landed gentry here, what separated the new United States from its European ancestors was the notion of equality for the common person. Brother Jonathan was the common man. Very common. He was unsophisticated, uneducated and unpolished. He was a hick. A hayseed. Poor, awkward and notoriously unsuccessful with women. But, according to Russell Nye, in *The Unembarrassed Muse*, he was "honest, shrewd, sentimental, independent, and possessed of a heart of gold." America's image of itself!

Brother Jonathan was the symbol of America in political cartoons on both sides of the Atlantic in the late 18th and early- to mid-19th centuries just as Uncle Sam is today. Brother Jonathan was also a familiar character in stage comedies of the day. The audiences knew the character and knew that this bumpkin would provide laughs throughout the play, yet somehow outwit and best those who had tried to take advantage of him. Think of Brother Jonathan as a rural Columbo detective figure, bumbling along in an unsophisticated way yet inevitably coming out ahead of the smart set!

Brother Jonathan's debut in political cartoons was in 1776, and he was featured in stage comedies beginning in 1787.

Over time, Brother Jonathan took on a recognizable costume of red-and-white striped overalls and a blue vest with white stars, a uniform he bequeathed to his successor, Uncle Sam. The Brother Jonathan figure was already on the wane when the Civil War came along. America was no longer so backward, and the common man with full voting rights was no longer so unthinkable. America was ready for an updated image. Maturity replaced youth. A knowing parent replaced the trouble-making youth. In short, America's new symbol was very much like Abraham Lincoln, the familiar father figure who had weathered the crisis of America's coming of age with wisdom and sternness.

There is a certain irony in the Brother Jonathan symbol lending its name to the Jonathan Club, since Brother Jonathan was the cultural opposite of the educated, well-dressed club member. But Brother Jonathan reflects the patriotic, not social, aspect of the caricature.

Where did this national symbol, Brother Jonathan, get his name? Simply from the fact that Jonathan was the "default" New England name just as John is today:

> *John Doe*
> *John Law*
> *John Q. Public*
> *Johnny come lately*
> *Dear John letter*
> *Prostitutes and their Johns*
> *The John in the back of the house*
> *When Johnny comes marching home again*

In puritan New England of Colonial times, "Brother" was a common honorific. Even more important, perhaps, was the fact that Masons referred to their fellow members as "Brother."

BROTHER JONATHAN AND JONATHAN TRUMBULL
(No relation)

In 1894, when the founders of the original Jonathan Club chose a name, they probably believed a link existed between Brother Jonathan and the Revolutionary War governor of Connecticut, Jonathan Trumbull. George Washington was supposed to have said, "Let us consult Brother Jonathan," or "Leave it to Brother Jonathan," or words to that effect. This notion has since been dispelled by scholars who traced the folklore to a Norwich, Connecticut, newspaper which, in 1846, published a claim by a man then in his 80s that the familiar Brother Jonathan character derived from Gov. Jonathan Trumbull. This was 71 years after Washington took command, 47 years after the death of Washington and 61 years after the death of Jonathan Trumbull. Neither Washington nor Trumbull nor any of their contemporaries mentioned this supposed connection. The man quoted (we don't even know his name!) would have been around nine years old during the American Revolution. The Norwich article was widely reprinted, leading to the myth that Brother Jonathan was a character based on Jonathan Trumbull.

Alice Wayland, Town Historian of Trumbull's hometown, Lebanon, Connecticut, said, "The belief that General George Washington referred to Governor Trumbull as 'Brother Jonathan' has taken root so deeply in popular culture that it is doubtful if scholarly works…can eradicate it from the public's mind. This is particularly true in Connecticut and even more so in Lebanon…with the quote attributed to General Washington used to illustrate the high esteem in which Trumbull was held by the father of our country."

While there are many mentions of Brother Jonathan in early newspaper accounts of the Club, there are no mentions of Jonathan Trumbull. When the Club commissioned a drawing of the personification of the Los Angeles Jonathan Club to send to Admiral Dewey in 1898, the members depicted Brother Jonathan, not Jonathan Trumbull.

The analogy of Uncle Sam might be helpful. Today we know that this fictional character was named for a real person, Sam Wilson, a meat packer in Troy, New York. Yet we think about the national symbol when we talk of Uncle Sam, not of the historic namesake, Sam Wilson. Thus, even though founding member Ed Tufts may well have believed that Brother Jonathan traced back to Gov. Trumbull, he probably had the patriotic symbol in mind when he suggested Brother Jonathan as the namesake for the new club.

When The Jonathan Club sent its well wishes to Admiral Dewey during the 1898 Spanish-American War, it did so with a representation of the Jonathan name. The Club commissioned a drawing of an idealized Brother Jonathan with a Jonathan Club banner and a 46-star American flag. This drawing is important because it telegraphs how the early members portrayed their club's namesake. Although the artist captured the Brother Jonathan icon's youth and longish hair, he portrayed a cleaned-up young gentleman befitting the exclusive club he was drawn to represent, instead of the familiar unsophisticated hayseed national character. The drawing's credit says it was "drawn by Chapin, from a photograph by Marceau." It is significant that the Club leaders personified their organization with Brother Jonathan, and not the Jonathan Trumbull figure that would become significant to the Club in later years.

A SOCIAL CLUB IS CHARTERED - 1895

While the political focus of the 1894 Jonathan Club was on state elections, the newspaper accounts focused far more on the club's social events. Non-political entertainment was important from the club's very founding, and the organization had soon settled into a schedule of regular Saturday night socials. It's little surprise then that after the elections of 1894 the Club members recognized that their real bond was social, not political, and re-formed themselves into a state-chartered social, non-political organization. (Even at the risk of admitting Democrats, God forbid!) The first meeting to discuss incorporating as a social club was held on June 8, 1895. It was about this time that Col. W. H. Chamberlain resigned as president because he was moving away from the city due to his wife's health. We don't know who took over the post from Chamberlain. Perhaps it was George Alexander, since the club members chose Alexander as president of the new social club.

The Club was chartered by the State of California on September 23, 1895, as "purely a social club without political, sporting or other special proclivities" according to a club brochure. The Club's quarters remained in the building at 130 South Spring Street and the new club kept most of the officers and directors. The members thought seriously about changing the name of their club. "Los Angeles Club" was the name they favored for a while, but ultimately they decided to keep the name of the 1894 Republican club. John Bushnell, a charter member, said in later years that the choice between Los Angeles Club and Jonathan Club was tested with the mailing of a letter from New York with no address other than "Jonathan Club." Ten days later the letter arrived, bearing the notation on its envelope, "Try Los Angeles." Bushnell said that that settled the matter "as the members realized the name was an original one."

132 South Spring Street

From 1896 until 1905, The Jonathan Club was headquartered above the retail space of Nicoll the Tailor and the Tufts-Lyon Arms Co. sporting goods store, both of whose names have been crudely painted over in this photograph from the 1900 Club roster. The Jonathan Club occupied the upper three floors, space that had been built out for the Corfu Hotel.

There were already at least three prominent social clubs in the city, the Los Angeles Athletic Club, founded in 1880, the California Club, founded in 1887 and the Union League Club of Los Angeles founded in 1889. The thought of the original members, as reported in their later years, was to start a club of young successful men in the city and grow old together as friends. The original board was composed of men in their 20s and 30s with a few token oldies in their early 40s. A Club brochure of the late 1890s described the Jonathan Club's niche among local organizations: "Every club has its own sphere to fill and the membership of the Jonathan is made up largely of the younger business and professional men – the active spirits who within the next twenty years are likely to carve out a considerable part of the destiny of Los Angeles."

In March of 1896, about six months after becoming a social organization, the Club moved one door south to 132 South Spring, from a two-story building to a four-story building.

The new Club space had formerly been the Corfu Hotel, which made it ideal for a club. It had a large dining space, kitchen, meeting rooms and overnight rooms. The Club occupied the entire second, third and fourth stories of what it always called "the Corfu Block" or "Corfu Building." Some of the members advanced $19,000 to fit out the new quarters.

Within a few years the membership had grown to almost 400.

The new club continued the tradition of the predecessor Republican Jonathan Club by staging entertainment events every Saturday night, featuring "the best talent from theater and opera." During the first few years of its existence the club teetered on the brink of going under on account of its severe money problems. General Harrison Gray Otis, the owner of the *Los Angeles Times*, "came repeatedly" to the Club's aid, saving the young organization from going "down and out."

GEORGE L. ALEXANDER

The Club's first president

The founding president of the social club was George L. Alexander (1865 – 1913). Years later Jonathan Club materials would claim that this George Alexander was elected mayor of Los Angeles, but this is not true. A different George Alexander (1839 – 1923) was the city's mayor. The Jonathan Club's George Alexander was the local manager for American Type Founders Company, which had transferred him here from Philadelphia. He didn't leave very distinct footprints as the Club's president and was replaced in The Jonathan Club's second year. In 1898 his company moved him to Portland, Oregon, and later to San Francisco, where he was the firm's Pacific Coast manager. He was killed in an automobile accident on August 19, 1913, at the age of 48.

Alexander's portrait was painted in about 1905 by one of Southern California's most famous artists of the day, Hanson Duvall Puthuff.

Rule's portrait was commissioned by the board of directors immediately following his death in 1908. The board paid portraitist John William Clawson $500 to paint the portrait from a photograph.

FERD K. RULE

He put the young Jonathan Club on its feet

Ferdinand K. Rule was the Club's president for eight years, from 1896 until 1904. It was he who put the Club on its feet, inspired its growth and stabilized it financially during the challenges of its early years. He was elected president shortly after the Club had moved from its original quarters to the larger spaces at 132 South Spring Street and was succeeded in 1904 by Henry Edwards Huntington shortly before the Club moved to the Pacific Electric Building. Even then, Ferd Rule was a Vice President, and may have continued to run the Club, since Huntington did not devote a great amount of time to his leadership post.

Ferd Rule was a leader of a variety of Los Angeles institutions. He was president of the La Fiesta de Los Angeles, a major annual event analogous to today's Pasadena Tournament of Roses. He was also president of the Los Angeles Chamber of Commerce and was prominent in Republican politics. In 1905 he resigned from the Salt Lake Railroad to go into the insurance business with his sons, O. Rey Rule and Gerald A. Rule. He died three years later, in 1908.

The Rule Company handled the insurance of the Jonathan Club for decades. Two other Jonathan Club presidents have headed that firm over the years. Warren Cleary, who was president in 1973-74, was president of the Rule company and as this book is written its chairman and CEO is another Jonathan Club past president, Bob Clemo.

- 1894 — The Jonathan Club, Republican support group, formed on April 30
- 1895 — The Jonathan Club chartered as social, non-political group, Sept. 23
- 1896 — Republicans nominate Ohio Gov. William McKinley in June. He wins Presidential election in November
- 1896 — Ford Rule elected Club president; begins 8-year term
- 1897 — First automobile in Los Angeles
- 1898 — L.A.'s first steel structure: Homer Laughlin Building
- 1898 — Battleship USS Maine blown up at Havana. Spanish-American War begins
- 1900 — Los Angeles population is 170,298
- 1901 — President McKinley assassinated
- 1902 — Henry E. Huntington moves to Los Angeles; joins The Jonathan Club and other clubs
- 1903 — Wright Brothers' flight

The Reading Room

The Reception Room

The Foyer

The Smoking Room

The Dining Room

The Billiard Room

Eleven young men
FOUNDING FATHERS OF THE JONATHAN CLUB

When The Jonathan Club segued from a Republican club into a non-partisan social club in 1895, its first board of directors posed for this historic photo. It is clear from this picture that what set this club apart was its youth. These were young men, already successful in the exploding town of Los Angeles, who wanted to forge friendships that would carry into their later years.

1. BENJAMIN F. DAY
Director,
Music Store Executive

B. F. Day was treasurer of the Southern California Music company. There had been a Day's Music store in downtown Los Angeles since the days when there were only a few stores in this frontier town. In time, the store merged with another music store to form Southern California Music Company.

6. FERD K. RULE
Second Vice President,
Auditor
L.A. Terminal Railway

Ferd Rule, at 42 years of age, was one of the old men of the group. He had come here from Kansas City to recover his health after work-related stress. He spent a year recuperating before going back to work. At the time of this picture he was auditor for the Los Angeles Terminal Railroad Company and he later became its general manager.

2. BRADNER W. LEE
Director,
Attorney

Bradner Lee, 45, was an attorney who became very prominent as he grew older. From the year after this photo was taken, and for many years, he served as chairman of the Republican County Central Committee. He was offered a judgeship, which he declined. Among the legal matters he is known for is handling the estate of Lucky Baldwin. Among the eleven men in this photo, the attorney was the only one with a telephone. Wouldn't you know it?

3. GEORGE P. TAYLOR
Director,
Tailor

George Taylor was, appropriately, a tailor. He had come here from New York a few years earlier. He was a tailor throughout his life.

4. GEORGE C. GASKILL
Director,
Agent for Tea and Mattings

George Gaskill was the agent of a company that sold teas and mattings (materials for making mats).

5. E.M. BURGOYNE
Secretary,
Post Office Clerk

E. M. Burgoyne, the Club's first secretary, was a clerk in the post office.

7. JOHN B. BUSHNELL
Vice President,
Railroad Executive

John Bushnell, 30, started off in the railroad business. He then became a very successful stockbroker. His father was a contractor who constructed most of the lighthouses around the Great Lakes.

8. GEORGE L. ALEXANDER
President,
Agent for Type Foundry

George Alexander, 29, the Club's first president, was the local agent for a type foundry company, selling equipment to printers.

11. CHARLES WHITE
Treasurer,
Ticket Agent for Railroad

C.H. White, the Club's original Treasurer, was the city ticket agent for the Southern Pacific Railroad, the number two person for the railroad in Los Angeles

9. HANCOCK BANNING
Director,
Capitalist

Hancock Banning, 30, was the most prominent of the first board members. His father, Phineas Banning, was one of the English-speaking pioneers of Southern California, founding the city of Wilmington and the port. Among the family's real estate holdings was Catalina Island, which it sold in 1919 to the Wrigleys. His occupation was listed as "Capitalist."

10. EDWARD B. TUFTS
Director,
Owner of Sporting Goods
and Bicycle Shop

Edward B. Tufts, 28, was a partner of the sporting goods store on the ground floor of The Jonathan Club's building at 132 S. Spring, the Tufts-Lyon Arms Co. Ed Tufts brought serious golf to Southern California. When he started his movement there was only one golf course in Los Angeles … on a vacant lot on 16th Street … a course with tomato cans and no grass. He established the first Los Angeles golf club, known today as the Los Angeles Country Club, and oversaw the Southern California Golf Association, watching golf in Southern California increase to 65 courses under his leadership. Incidentally, it was Ed Tufts who came up with the name The Jonathan Club.

Chapter 2
Pacific Electric Building

- 1904 – Henry Edwards Huntington elected president of Club, begins 8-year term
- 1905 – Club moves to Pacific Electric Building, 6th and Main
- 1906 – San Francisco earthquake
- 1910 – Los Angeles population: 310,198
- 1914 – First Jonathan Club barber shop
- 1915 – Jonathan Club member, A.C. Bicke, dies in sinking of the Lusitania
- 1916 – First manicurist hired "for gentlemen and ladies"
- 1916 – Shoeshine service added to barber shop
- 1916 – Telegraphic service arranged to provide results of Presidential election
- 1916 – *The Jonathan* magazine debuts

THE MOVE FROM 132 SPRING STREET

The Huntington Years

By 1902, the Club had established itself as a prestigious organization of business and professional men. Its founders were seven years older now, so the club had lost its focus on youth, although its membership was still younger that that of the competing California Club.

The Jonathan Club had long since shed its Republican partisanship, although its members were still individually involved in Republican politics. The Club membership had swelled to 360 members and had outgrown its quarters at 132 South Spring Street. It was time for a change.

Enter Henry Edwards Huntington. We know him today as Henry Huntington, but during his lifetime his family and closest friends called him Ed or Edwards. To most of the world he was Mr. Huntington.

In 1902, Huntington (1) settled in Southern California, (2) joined the Jonathan Club, (3) planned his Pacific Electric Building and (4) offered the top two floors to the California Club, and later to the Jonathan Club. Busy year.

Huntington bought land in a residential district away from downtown for a headquarters building for his Pacific Electric Company, at the corner of Sixth and Main Streets. He bet on the fact that the business community and the U.S. Post Office would gravitate towards his location since it was to be the city's transportation hub. He was right.

After his architect, Thornton Fitzhugh, had designed the nine-story colossus, Huntington suggested modifying the top two floors for use as a private club, and he invited the California Club, to which he belonged, to move into his building. But the timing was bad for the California Club, since it had already committed to move from shared quarters at Spring and Second Streets to its own building at Hill and Fifth Streets. So, Huntington offered the space to The Jonathan Club, for which the timing was perfect. The Jonathan Club decided to take this immense leap from its small quarters on Spring Street despite the fact that the club had only 360 members.

The architect went to work immediately on the difficult job of modifying two floors already divided up into office space, for use as a private club. The grateful Jonathan Club elected Mr. Huntington its president.

A scandal surrounded that election. Ferd Rule's eight-year leadership of the Club had been appreciated by most, but not all, of the membership, and Rule had declined to run for reelection as president. He did agree to run for the Board again. A ballot was drafted suggesting Mr. Huntington as president and Ferd Rule as a director. A rival ballot was proposed, also with Mr. Huntington as president, substituting a member of the nominating committee for Ferd Rule as director, but this maneuver was rebuked in the press and was dropped.

By August of 1903, the plans for the new Jonathan Club had been completed. Huntington offered the Club a ten-year lease at $400 a month. In 1915 the rent was raised to $1,000 a month for another ten-year term.

On June 17, 1904, a general membership meeting was held to give members a tour of their new Club home and to approve the financing method. The membership okayed issuing bonds for $50,000 at 5 percent (later changed to 6 percent), maturing in not more than ten years, to be subscribed by Club members. The total cost of furnishing the new quarters came to $60,000 to $70,000.

The Jonathan Club retained about a thousand dollars' worth of effects from its headquarters at 132 South Spring Street. The directors voted to accept an offer to sell the remaining effects for $4,500 to the new tenant, the Occidental Club, but reversed themselves at their next meeting and decided to put the Club's contents up for auction. A newspaper article described the auction as a strange scene, with the rank and file of society trooping through spaces that had heretofore been off limits to all but members and their carefully invited guests. The Jonathan Club auction brought in $4,226, much of it from the agents of the Occidental Club. Within a year the Occidental Club would fail and the same effects would be put up for auction once again.

The Club moved in on March 15, 1905. The opening of the new quarters was a lavish affair. In gratitude to the police chief for furnishing officers to deal with the event the Board voted to give $25 to the chief, "to be used as he sees fit." To cope with the additional expenses of the Club's elegant new digs, dues were raised to $5 a month. The daily luncheon price at the Club at that time was 50 cents.

A special reception was held for Mr. Huntington on June 21, at which the great man shook hands and chatted with members of the Club that he housed in his building and which he oversaw, in a ceremonial way, as its president.

Timeline:
- 1917 – U.S. enters World War I
- 1918 – *The Jonathan* magazine folds
- 1918 – World War I Armistice signed
- 1919 – *The Jonathan* magazine re-started
- 1920 – Los Angeles population: 576,673
- 1920 – Prohibition begins
- 1920 – Women given the right to vote
- 1922 – First local commercial radio stations: KFI, KNX, KHJ
- 1923 – First sound-on-film motion picture
- 1923 – William Jeffries elected JC President; land purchased at 6th and Figueroa; architect Schultze & Weaver hired

The Club was in its Pacific Electric Building location during World War I. One of the precipitating factors for America's entry in the war was the German sinking of the Steamer *Lusitania*. A Jonathan Club member, A. C. Bilicke, lost his life in that May 7, 1915, tragedy.

The strange club that moved into The Jonathan Club's old quarters

In 1896, The Jonathan Club moved into the space of the late Corfu Hotel at 132 South Spring Street. When the Club moved out nine years later the building was still known as the "Corfu Building."

In 1905, when the Jonathan Club left Spring Street and moved into the new Pacific Electric Building at Sixth and Main, another club moved into the quarters that The Jonathan Club had made famous. This replacement club could hardly have been more different. The new club was the Occidental Club, surely one of the most bizarre clubs in Southern California history.

The Occidental Club was started by George Noble Todd, who offered to buy the Arcadia Hotel on the beach in Santa Monica. The new Occidental Club was to have parallel cement archways extending 300 feet into the ocean, connected at their offshore ends with "turbines or water wheels" to break the force of the waves and create a giant pool of calm ocean for the club guests. On the piers into the ocean were to be "a fine promenade, ocean chutes, cafes, and various amusement features for the exclusive use of the club members and their guests."

Occidental Club members not only would get use of a club of unbelievable luxury which extended into the ocean itself, but would become co-owners of the Arcadia Hotel and other properties of the Occidental Investment Company organized by the same Mr. Todd. Each member's dues were to be non-assessable shares, which were to benefit from all of the assets but none of the liabilities of the many real estate holdings. Commissioned brokers sold the club memberships, taking 40 percent of each sale.

Mr. Todd's negotiations to purchase the Arcadia Hotel fell through, and a revolution of angry members erupted. The Occidental Club, scrambling to find new quarters, contracted for the space being vacated by The Jonathan Club and attended the Jonathan Club's public auction to buy many of the furnishings that The Jonathan Club had declined to sell it directly.

The troubled Occidental Club was to suffer even more crises. Soon after moving in, its members attacked one of the staff members who turned out the lights at midnight as he had been instructed. Indignant card players, including a professional boxer, beat the staff member senseless, as other club members cheered the attackers on. The steward died of his injuries a month later, prompting a brouhaha in the press. The disreputable Occidental Club at first stood behind its members, only reluctantly bowing to pressure and finally expelling the thugs. (It bears repeating that this abominable club had no connection whatsoever with The Jonathan Club).

How could the Occidental Club escape its latest controversy? The Occidental Club's board took quick and decisive action: The board members changed their name to throw off the unwanted criticism, becoming the Commercial Club. The Arcadia Hotel was suing the club for ruining its season's business, members were apoplectic about the disappearance of the club's money and the club was now having to fend off the worst kind of publicity. The Commercial Club soon collapsed completely.

The Jonathan Club by then was enjoying new success at the top of one of the world's largest office buildings.

The Main Ballroom (also called the Amusement Room) was the largest space in The Jonathan Club's Pacific Electric quarters. The stage could be removed, depending on the use of the room. Creating a ballroom out of space already partially constructed as offices was a special problem for architect Thornton Fitzhugh. According to notes of the architect, "The musicians gallery and the deep semicircular ribs are devices for overcoming acoustic difficulties of a concrete vault." The notes on this photograph point out that everything visible in the picture above the floor (except the seats) is concrete. The notes say "French sash to left opens to balcony overlooking roof-garden - accessible by hand made iron stairs simulating work seen in the early Californian architecture."

The lobby of the club, on the eighth floor, extended up through the ninth floor to a colored glass dome overhead (upper two photos). The showpiece of the lobby, and the Club, was a marble statue, "The Combatants," sculpted by Cattalucci. Today the statue guards the south end of the Town Club swimming pool.

The Reading Room of the Pacific Electric Jonathan Club included dark cloisonné metal vases that sit in the Town Club's Reading Room a century later. The architect created this nook "to segregate a portion of the great room 42 x 70 feet and to minimize the cheerless effect of so large a room."

One of the most distinguished features of The Jonathan Club at the Pacific Electric Building was its eighth floor roof garden. The Club occupied the eighth and ninth floors of the building.

Employees of The Jonathan Club circa 1905

Four fireplaces masked the main smokestack for the building in the Conversation Room. The divans hid the fireplaces in the summer and were turned to face them in the winter. The architect said, "This illustrates one of the many difficulties in converting the already partly created office building to club purposes. The false wall and double arches to the left were used to bring the stack and its fireplaces to the center of the room."

The bar was designed as an English tap room, with a light wall of broken champagne bottles set in lead and other walls of 15 foot-high oak panels sporting a plate rail with burning candles. The beer stein collection in the 1925 Grill Room and today's Tap Room collection traces back to the steins in this bar. Today's Town Club Tap Room also uses the motif of broken champagne bottles.

Old English Tap Room

The detail on the stage's proscenium centers on the Club's initials, "J.C."

Tracks ran completely through the Pacific Electric Building, with a full train station inside the building. Note the trolley pulling onto Main Street in the postcard photo above.

The east side of the Pacific Electric Building.

PACIFIC ELECTRIC BUILDING

The Club's third home

When it was finished in 1905, the Pacific Electric Building was a Los Angeles marvel. It was nine stories high–the largest office building in the world, exceeding the Broad Exchange in New York which had held the record until then.

Huntington had chosen a site at Main and Sixth Streets in a residential neighborhood well south of the downtown area at the time. He led, or anticipated, the growth of downtown in that direction.

His building, known locally as the Huntington Building, contained 12 acres of office space and almost five miles of corridors and stairways. Its first floor, with 30-foot ceilings, was a passenger terminal with platforms on both sides of the double tracks that ran through the building from east to west. The passenger waiting room, the size of a city lot, was adjoined by the largest dining room in Los Angeles and a separate lunch room.

Large offices occupied each of the six office floors above, served by corridors eight feet wide. The smallest of the offices were 300 square feet and the largest were 4,800 square feet in size.

Its vast basement was empty, awaiting the laying of tracks for the freight franchise that Huntington had thus far been unable to secure.

The seventh floor was occupied by the Pacific Electric Company itself and divided into 99 offices.

The top two floors of this showpiece were occupied by The Jonathan Club. The *Los Angeles Examiner* wrote, "It is doubtful that if a similar organization anywhere in the world has more beautiful and more perfectly appointed quarters." Two of the building's six elevators served The Jonathan Club exclusively.

The visitor left the elevator on the eighth floor to enter a vestibule, about 20 feet square, and proceed through plate glass doors into a two-story rotunda topped by a dome of colored glass 45 feet up. The rotunda, 100 feet by 50 feet, was guarded by eight solid marble columns, surrounding a marble sculpture familiar to Jonathan Club members today, Cattalucci's "The Combatants," which now sits at one end of the Town Club swimming pool. A grand marble staircase led to the ninth floor. The lobby was intended to be a facsimile of the Congressional Library in Washington D.C.

On the ninth floor was the ornate ball room, "a room fit for a prince's fete," according to the *Los Angeles Examiner*. The room was free of columns, boasted a 45-foot ceiling and had a movable stage at one end for "vaudeville entertainments."

The Reading Room was 100 feet long and 50 feet wide faced by a fireplace large enough for a five-foot log. Nearby was a large conversation room.

The Club spaces featured a roof garden on the eighth floor, decked out with blooming flowers and climbing vines. From this floor the ocean could be viewed in two different directions, and, on a clear day, Catalina Island.

The Jonathan Club contained a number of residential rooms. How many? It's hard to know. The *Los Angeles Herald* said 47, the *Los Angeles Times* said 52, the *Los Angeles Examiner* said 60 and *Leslie's Weekly* said "more than 60."

A gymnasium measuring 50x20 feet was adjoined by "shower baths in abundance," according to the *Los Angeles Examiner*. The Turkish room was "elliptical in every dimension, except the floor, which is level only of necessity." The ceiling had a colored glass skylight. Off the Turkish room, painted red, was the billiard room, painted green, with nine tables and room for as many more. A card room, also painted green, lay off the billiard room.

No woman was allowed on the Club elevators to the eighth and ninth floors. She was required to exit on the seventh floor, walk down a block-long corridor, enter through what was called "the secret entrance," up a narrow stairway to a little booth where a "matron" checked her credentials and allowed her to pass into the women's reception room. "Here she will find all the requisites necessary to the complete toilet of the woman of the most fastidious tastes," said the *Los Angeles Examiner*. When ready, she then entered the main hall to meet her escort, who had, of course, simply ridden up on the elevator. The women's area on the eighth floor contained a large dining room and three private dining rooms.

This construction photo is dramatic proof that Huntington built his headquarters in a residential neighborhood. He built south of the existing business district on less expensive real estate knowing that if he made his building the transportation hub the business district and the U.S. Post Office would have to come his way.

Far beneath the serene activities of The Jonathan Club was a hubbub of activity in the Pacific Electric passenger terminal on the first floor of the Pacific Electric Building.

John Willard Clawson (1858-1936)
Portrait of Henry E. Huntington
Oil on canvas, Jonathan Club #676

The board of directors commissioned this portrait of Huntington in 1907, budgeting $500 for the portraitist John Willard Clawson. Clawson was a grandson of Brigham Young. His studio was destroyed in the 1906 fire in San Francisco. He moved to Los Angeles, where he stayed until 1933.

Henry Edwards Huntington lived at The Jonathan Club in a five-room, two-bath suite. These are views of his home in the Club.

Henry Edwards Huntington

Henry Edwards Huntington was one of the wealthiest, most powerful people in Southern California. As one of the region's largest employers, he provided jobs to 5,000 workers. He owned the regional transportation system, and he owned important utilities, as well, including Pacific Light and Power, which was the largest hydroelectric supplier in the region and a provider of natural gas. He also owned the San Gabriel Valley Water Company.

Mr. Huntington shaped the future of Southern California more than did any other individual. He oversaw the spider-web empire of the Pacific Electric Company, the largest interurban rail operation in the world, with 1,000 miles of track and over 900 railcars. Huntington is known today for his railway empire, but that's not where he made his fortune. His trolleys were simply a means to his end of real estate development. Huntington bought massive parcels of outlying land, which were made valuable by his railway connections.

In a time when the Los Angeles County planning department was weak, Huntington shaped the region, deciding where towns would be built, and whether they would be communities for the working classes, middle classes or the gentry. It was to his advantage to spread the population out along his trolley lines, therefore Los Angeles did not expand evenly outward from a strong central core, like in other cities, but as

far-flung strings of pearls throughout the region. Southern California today is still largely a creation of Huntington's. The rail routes he dreamed up yesterday are, to some degree, the freeway routes of today. The socioeconomic plans he conceived for various local communities remain locked in a hundred years later.

Huntington was born in 1850, to a family of modest means, in Oneonta, New York. He worked in his father's general store and in a department store and he managed a sawmill before coming under the sponsorship of his uncle, Collis P. Huntington, one of the "Big Four" of California (along with Charles Crocker, Mark Hopkins and Leland Stanford). Uncle Collis tested young Henry Edwards at ever-increasing levels of responsibility, ultimately bringing him to San Francisco to help him run the Southern Pacific Company.

Henry Edwards Huntington saw huge potential in Southern California and focused his energy on the opportunities around Los Angeles. Huntington said, "I am a farsighted man, and I believe that Los Angeles is destined to become the most important city in this country if not in the world. It can extend in any direction as far as you like." He also said, "We of the Pacific Electric Railway will join this whole region into one big family."

He established himself locally in 1902 and immediately joined The Jonathan Club, California Club and a number of other local clubs. Although Huntington was a business loner he served on as many as 60 boards of directors at any one time, and was a member of dozens of private clubs. He stayed in the Metropolitan Club while in New York and when he was in Southern California he lived in a private five-room/two-bath suite in The Jonathan Club. He continued to stay at the Club even after the 1910 construction of his 550-acre San Marino estate, until he remarried in 1913. It was much easier for him to take an elevator home than to make the trek to San Marino, even though he had a private trolley car, the 100 mph "Alabama" that could deliver him home on a private track.

Huntington was elected president of The Jonathan Club in 1904 and presided over a number of board meetings. He tried to resign in early 1905, just as the Club was moving into its new quarters in his building, but The Jonathan Club board members talked him out of it, perhaps assuring him that his name at the top of the letterhead was what was wanted, even if he could not attend meetings. He remained president for 12 years, until 1916, the longest rein of any the Club's presidents, but he was not actively involved in the Club affairs. He did not attend any board meetings during his last six years as president, and other board members did the heavy lifting during that period. At first this duty fell to Ferd Rule, who had been president for the previous eight years. Later, prominent architect John Austin served that function for a number of years, and was rewarded by being elected to the presidency in his own right for the years 1916-1917, succeeding Huntington.

Between 1914 and 1917, Huntington withdrew from business interests and spent more and more time collecting rare books and paintings. In 1919, he established The Huntington Library, Art Collections, and Botanical Gardens so that the public could enjoy his massive collection of British and American books and documents, art and unusual plants.

In 1916, the Club finally recognized that Huntington was not actively involved in the leadership of the Club and that the pretense should be dropped. Nevertheless, they named Huntington Honorary President for Life, "in recognition of his services and devotion to this Club and the many and great benefits conferred on it by him."

Henry Edwards Huntington died in 1927, two years after the completion of the new Jonathan Club at Sixth and Figueroa Streets. The Club hung black crepe around his portrait and flew its flags at half mast for two weeks, to honor the man who had figured so importantly in the Club's history.

STORIES AT THE PACIFIC ELECTRIC BUILDING

The avocado industry of Southern California began at The Jonathan Club

Shortly after the Jonathan Club moved into its new quarters in the Pacific Electric Building, Henry Huntington became fascinated by a fruit served up by the Club's chef. The chef had obtained the fruit from a farm in Atlixco in the state of Puebla, Mexico. Huntington collected the seeds at his table and asked the chef for others, then took the lot to William Hertrich, the executive gardener at his San Marino estate. The chef had told him the fruit was an "alligator pear," but Hertrich recognized the fruit as "ahuacate," also known as "avocado." At Huntington's request Hertrich grew the seeds in pots until hundreds of the young seedlings could be planted. Eventually, seven acres of avocado plants were growing at Huntington's ranch, and the avocado industry of Southern California was born.

Hertrich, the man famous today for designing the Huntington Gardens, was a charter member of the California Avocado Association, formed in 1915 in Los Angeles, and he wrote extensively on the fruit. He participated in the formation of the City of San Marino and was elected to its school board and city council.

Some of the avocado trees that grew from those original Jonathan Club seeds are still producing fruit today at the Huntington Gardens.

The day police raided the California Club

The early afternoon of September 22, 1908, is one that the California Club will never forget. That was the day its entire board of directors was arrested.

A phalanx of policemen in "Keystone Kops helmets" burst into the stately club with city prosecutor Thomas Lee Woolwine in a raid timed for when the club would be most crowded. The cops shuffled through plush carpets to the barroom, which was locked. Lieutenant Charles Dixon, the ranking police officer, ordered the door broken down. The cops were ready to comply, until a bystanding club member, Charles Monroe, who just happened to be a Superior Court judge, asked the cops to wait, noting that the manager had been called to bring the keys.

The police party scooped up rare glassware, expensive champagne and fine wines as evidence, taking a bartender and the club manager into custody.

Some of the women dining at the Club's ladies' annex fled in terror, supposing that all present would be arrested. The men, however, quit their whist and billiard games to watch the events unfold with morbid fascination. What irked some of the members more than the raid, even, was that one of the cops availed himself of the food laid out for the luncheon hour. "Policeman Stays to Lunch" proclaimed the *Los Angeles Examiner*.

The raid was prompted by a longstanding dispute between the City of Los Angeles and the private clubs as to whether the clubs needed retail liquor dealers licenses. Prosecutor Woolwine, a frequent visitor to the Californian Club, decided that a raid would impress the clubs with his seriousness.

It did. A director of The Jonathan Club contacted Woolwine that afternoon to say that The Jonathan Club would close down its bar until the matter had been resolved in court. In a special meeting of the board called the next day by club president Henry E. Huntington, it was ordered that "all rooms, ice boxes and closets containing wines and liquors" were to be "locked and sealed."

The law firm of Gibson, Trask, Dunn & Crutcher, representing the California Club and Jonathan Club, threatened to hold the raiding parties liable for damages. Ultimately, the California Supreme Court upheld the right of bona fide clubs to sell liquor to their members without being subject to laws requiring a municipal liquor license. The end came with a matter-of-fact court decision quite at variance with the raid that had made history with private clubs in Downtown Los Angeles on September 22, 1908.

The Strange Bonfilio Affair

On May 2, 1904, N. Bonfilio received more votes than did Henry Huntington, the new president, or Ferd Rule, the man who had been the president for virtually the entire life of the Club. Bonfilio was elected treasurer, was part of the small Furnishing Committee for the new quarters in the Pacific Electric Building and even traveled to the East Coast to arrange contracts for the new décor. His daughter, Millie Bonfilio, oversaw the immense job of decorating what was arguably the most spectacular club headquarters in the country, in an era when private clubs were far, far more numerous than today. She was recognized for her contribution in a major *Los Angeles Times* article. Her father had obviously spent an immense amount of time on a job that ultimately impressed members and outsiders alike.

The audit report after the Club's completion expressed the "everlasting gratitude of all the members of this Club" for bringing in the project under budget. At the general membership meeting, the members voted their praise for Miss Bonfilio and in the very next action voted her father out of office, apparently with the charge of financial irregularities. He submitted his resignation and asked for a full audit of the books to clear himself. Not only did the audit clear him completely, but a petition signed by about 100 members asked that he be given a life membership for his contributions to the Club. In a general meeting of the membership presided over by Mr. Huntington himself, signers of the petition withdrew their petition and the meeting ended. Clearly there is more to this than meets the eye. Information must have been shared with those who had signed the petition. His resignation was accepted at the next board meeting. Alas, we've yet to learn the full story a century later!

The Jonathan Club of Mexico

On February 16, 1922, a special meeting of the membership was called to consider a Jonathan Club facility in Mexico, just south of the border near a town called Tecate. Jonathan Club President George A. Charters explained that the Club had a thousand acres under option and that an additional thousand or fifteen hundred acres could be secured directly from the government of Mexico.

So that the Club would not go into debt for this venture, the initiation fee was raised from $100 to $250. Thus new memberships would cover the entire expense.

The members examined photographs of the new Jonathan Club site and voted unanimously to proceed with the venture. The members authorized the board of directors "to enter into and contract concessions; to organize a civil association under the laws of Mexico; to make and enter into leases; to purchase such land as may be necessary; and to make all other necessary expenditures of money to complete the plan as outlined by the president at this meeting." Olé!

What was the appeal of a Club branch in Mexico? Board minutes do not say exactly. Perhaps it had to do with Prohibition, which had been in effect for two years. Maybe the Jonathans were getting thirsty. The only attraction mentioned in the board minutes was the site's good hunting.

The Club dispatched a member of its board, Dr. Ray D. Robinson, to Mexico City to make the necessary arrangements. The Club president and another board member visited the site in Tecate and members of the Club were invited to inspect the facility on a field trip that would cost $20 each.

Evidently the trip did not go well, because a special membership meeting had to be called immediately to quell the sudden opposition to a project which had had Club support up to this point. In a board meeting immediately before the membership meeting, Dr. Robinson offered to buy the project from the Club if the members were against it. The members, who had voted unanimously for the project, now voted unanimously to sell the leases and entitlements to Dr. Robinson and be done with it.

The initiation fee was lowered from $250 back to $100, and those who had paid the higher fee in the interim got refunds of the difference.

Robinson had agreed to buy the entitlements on May 23, 1922. The board of directors minutes reflect an ongoing frustration at not being able to collect the promised money. For almost two years the directors pressured their fellow board member to resolve the matter. After one such discussion, Dr. Robinson resigned from the board. He finally paid the Club three years after offering to buy the rights.

The resort in Tecate, Mexico, kept the name Jonathan Country Club, but with the understanding that all "literature or publicity" would disclaim any connection with The Jonathan Club of Los Angeles.

UCLA was started at The Jonathan Club

UCLA was conceived one day in the fall of 1917 at The Jonathan Club in the Pacific Electric Building. Edward A. Dickson, the only Southern California member of the Board of Regents of the University of California, brought Ernest C. Moore to lunch that day. Moore was the new president of Los Angeles State Normal School on Vermont Avenue. Dickson's idea was to adopt Moore's institution as the Southern California branch of the University of California, with Moore as its chief executive.

The two battled against the entrenched establishment of Northern California, fighting through the halls of the state legislature and governor's office. Finally the university was formed on Moore's Vermont Avenue campus with Moore as its chief executive, just as the two had plotted at The Jonathan Club.

The Vermont location, always considered an interim solution, was abandoned after Dickson led a bond drive to purchase property in Westwood and to build an initial set of buildings: Royce Hall, Powell Library, Kinsey Hall and Haines Hall.

At the time of the historic Jonathan Club luncheon, Edward Dickson was 38 and was the political editor of the *Los Angeles Express*, a newspaper he later purchased. A graduate of the University of California in 1901, he served on the University of California Board of Regents for 43 years, longer than has any other individual. He was a Regent from the time he was 33 until he died at age 76.

Other Facilities Considered by The Jonathan Club

1912 – "1,035 acres for a playground"

1913 – Clubhouse at Big Pines

1914 – A facility in Mountain Home

1921 – A floating club house

1922 – Jonathan Country Club in Tecate, Mexico

1922 – Country club in Triunfo

1922 – "New club quarters" on the Ringe Estate

1927 – Club Site for fishing, swimming and boating in Holcomb Valley (The Edgewater Club was offered at the same board meeting)

1930 – Edgewater Club (which the Club bought)

1935 – Sea Breeze Club (which the Club bought)

At the Pacific Electric Building clubhouse elaborate "Hi-Jinks" stag parties were staged. This "barn" was constructed inside the ballroom, possibly in January 1909. There are no women in this picture; all the participants in this photograph are costumed male revelers. At the time of this party these costumes were from an era within the lifetime of many of the participants, so some of the "costumes" may well be the real things. The Club also held annual "Lo-Jinks" retreats to mountain resorts in such locations as Mountain Home, California.

Chapter 3
Sixth and Figueroa

- 1924 — Ground broken for Jonathan Club Town Club
- 1925 — Club moves to new Town Club at 6th and Figueroa
- 1925 — Edgewater Club opens in Santa Monica. It will become the Jonathan Beach Club in 1930
- 1926 — Revolving doors installed at Town Club entryway
- 1927 — Charles A. Lindbergh's solo flight across Atlantic

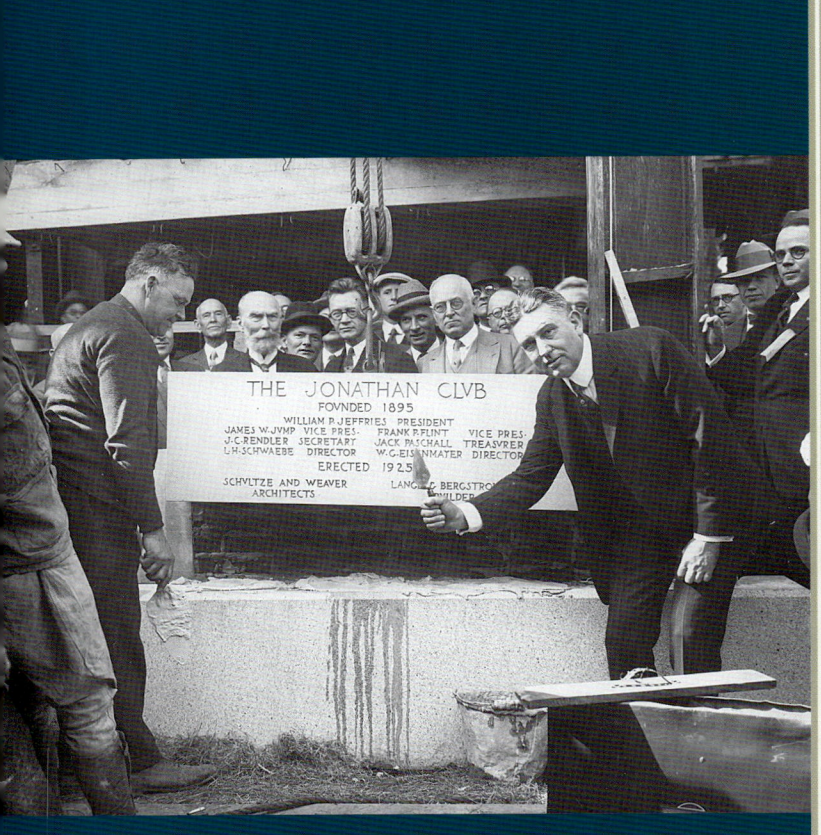

Club President William Jeffries uses a trowel to cement the cornerstone of the Town Club on February 26, 1925.

A HOME OF ITS OWN

The Club's lease at the Pacific Electric Building was set to expire in March of 1925, but by 1920 there were hints in the board minutes that the Club was beginning to feel constrained by its landlord. Henry E. Huntington, the man who had brought the Club there, had long since retreated from active involvement in the Club and was less and less active in the Pacific Electric company, as well. The board minutes refer to requests by the Club for different elevator arrangements, for using all or part of the garage exclusively for Club members' automobiles, modification of the roof garden and leasing the seventh floor as an extension of the Club's facilities on the eighth and ninth floors. One cryptic note in the board minutes says that "A letter was read from the Pacific Electric Ry., regarding the elimination of rats in the Club quarters…"

In late 1922, the board of directors began to explore the option of a dedicated home for The Jonathan Club. At the Town Club's dedication three years later, William Jeffries would credit Director James W. Jump for the idea of building a new Jonathan Club. In 1922, the board authorized the Club president, George A. Charters, and a director, J. W. Jump, "to make investigations of property located in the vicinity of Figueroa and Seventh streets and report results at next meeting of the Board." Thus the board not only was in a mood to move, but had in mind the specific neighborhood they were interested in. Over the past century, the downtown core had migrated in the form of a backwards "L" beginning in the area that would later be known for Olvera Street, inching south along Spring and Main and turning west along Seventh Street. Figueroa was the forward edge of Downtown Los Angeles' push.

1927 – Sea Breeze Club opens in Santa Monica. It will later become the Jonathan Beach Club in 1935.

1928 – City Hall building dedicated. Designed (with others) by former Jonathan Club president John Austin.

The Club felt out the Pacific Electric Railway's management on possible terms for a ten-year extension, but meanwhile its two-man committee reported that they had located "two or three" possible sites and were particularly interested in parcels at Fifth and Olive Streets and Orange and Figueroa Streets. They later expressed interest in a property on Grand Avenue between Sixth and Seventh.

Pacific Electric Railway officials said that they planned to remodel the entire building and that they could fetch $7,500 a month for office use on their eighth and nine floors, which was seven and a half times the $1,000 rent they were getting from The Jonathan Club. The Railway suggested a rent of $3,500 a month.

In May of 1923, William P. Jeffries was elected to the board and immediately chosen as the Club's new president. Never before or since has a member been elected to the president's role without a prior term on the board of directors. George A. Charters, who had served as president for the past three years, and who had just been re-elected to the board, resigned from the board almost immediately. The proposed replacement for Charters turned down the offer, and it took five months to fill the vacancy, by which time the treasurer had resigned. Charters remained active in the Club and served on the Furnishings Committee for the new facility.

Jeffries flew into his new post with immense energy and vision. Three days after his election he called for an immediate meeting with 100 selected members "to discuss in detail the plans for the future home of The Jonathan Club." The day after this private meeting, 150 members attended a special membership meeting. As would be the case throughout his tenure, Jeffries may have been leading faster than this flock wanted to follow. Some members argued that the Club should stay where it was. Ultimately, though, a motion that the board "be authorized to expend funds from the Treasury for option or purchase of property for future home of the Club" carried unanimously.

Within a month Jeffries had offered Mrs. Belle Fulton a 99-year lease on her property facing Seventh Street near Francisco Street. After Mrs. Fulton turned him down Jeffries made an offer to Burkhart Investment Company of $30,000 a month for a 99-year lease on property at the northwest corner of Sixth and Figueroa Streets. At a special meeting on July 19, 1923, only four members voted against going forward. Jeffries envisioned a $750,000 building. His vision would grow fourfold as momentum picked up, the building ultimately costing $3 million. A postcard poll of the membership was taken with 563 voting in favor of the move, 104 voting against and seven members undecided.

Jeffries wasted no time, and secured the Burkhard lease, not through the Club, but through his own Angeles Mesa Land Company, which earned $9,250 in commissions on the deal. Jeffries immediately turned over his commission to the Club. In November, only six months after his election, Jeffries had chosen Schultze and Weaver as the architect for the Club's new quarters, after "a careful consideration of a number of architects."

On February 14, 1924, Jeffries presented the plans of the new building at a meeting of the membership, "for its final approval or criticism." Architect Leonard Schultze "showed the new building through lantern slides." Mr. W. J. Arkell "among other things offered to donate a radio set to the Club for the new building to cost not less than $10,000."

The Club, under Jeffries, formed a corporation, Jonathan Club Building Company, for the purpose of acquiring the lease and assuming the obligation to construct its building. Subscriptions were held for first and second mortgage bonds, totaling $1,250,000 each. Jeffries himself subscribed to $65,000 of the First Mortgage Six and One-Half Percent Serial Gold Bonds, but later asked the Club to buy him out of $40,000 of his share. Rule & Sons, the insurance firm run by the son of the Club's second president, subscribed to the First Mortgage bonds as well, as did 13 banks and Pacific Mutual Life Insurance. (Board minutes Aug. 21, 1924) Second Mortgage Leasehold Seven Per Cent Serial Gold Bonds were sold largely to members, who were called "Red Star Men" in recognition of their participation.

The following firms were considered for the task of building the great new club:

The Davidson Construction Co.
Edwards, Wildey & Dixon
Lange & Bergstrom
Scofield Engineering Co.
Los Angeles Planning Mill Co.
McDonald & Kahn Co.
Pozzo Construction Co.
Simpson Construction Co.

The firm of Lange & Bergstrom was engaged to construct the building, for a contractor's fee of $2,167,488.00, with the commitment to complete the building within 15 months. Ultimately this schedule slipped and there was a dispute between the Club and architect on one side and the contractor on the other.

Ground was broken on August 4, 1924, before a group of about 150 members of The Jonathan Club. Architect Fullerton Weaver presented Jeffries with a golden spade inscribed with praise for "the stupendous task of making the dream of a new Jonathan Club House a brilliant reality." The inscription also noted that the "Shovel is mightier than the pen or sword." Jeffries himself turned the first soil, signaling the beginning of construction, then introduced John Bushnell, one of the original 1895 board members.

In August, the initiation fee was raised to $300 and the active member number set at 1,700. How the Club was growing! Only two years earlier the membership had been limited to 1,000.

The Southern California Telephone Company installed 300 lines and 15 trunks for the new Club building, and agreed to charge the Club a flat rate of $340 per month. Arthur E. Baker (sic), of Barker Brothers, was appointed the consulting decorator for the new club house at a fee of 2 percent of the total cost of "all furnishings upon which his advice was required."

The lease for the Pacific Electric Building expired on February 28, 1925, and the Club had to increase its rent payments from $1,000 to $3,500 per month until it could move to its new quarters. It provided for this increased rent by temporarily raising the monthly dues from $7 to $10.

The 15-month construction period, including the groundbreaking on August 24, 1924, was documented on silent film by Dwyer Studios. On February 26, 1925, the cornerstone was laid, to the accompaniment of the Jonathan Club Band and the Jonathan Club Glee Club, ten of the original members and 600 members and guests. Sealed in that cornerstone are 23 items, including a copy of the film shot at the groundbreaking and a copy of the first Club roster, printed in 1896.

During construction, on April 16, 1925, six huge stones weighing more than a ton came tumbling down from the third floor of the structure. Overdramatic initial reports indicated that the building had collapsed and six ambulances were dispatched immediately to the site. The stones struck a scaffold hurling a stonemason and his helper towards the ground. The stonemason managed to hang onto a ledge on the way down and the helper grabbed a rope and pulled himself to safety. One of the stones slightly injured the superintendent of construction who was standing on the ground. No one was seriously injured in the mishap, according to the *Los Angeles Times*.

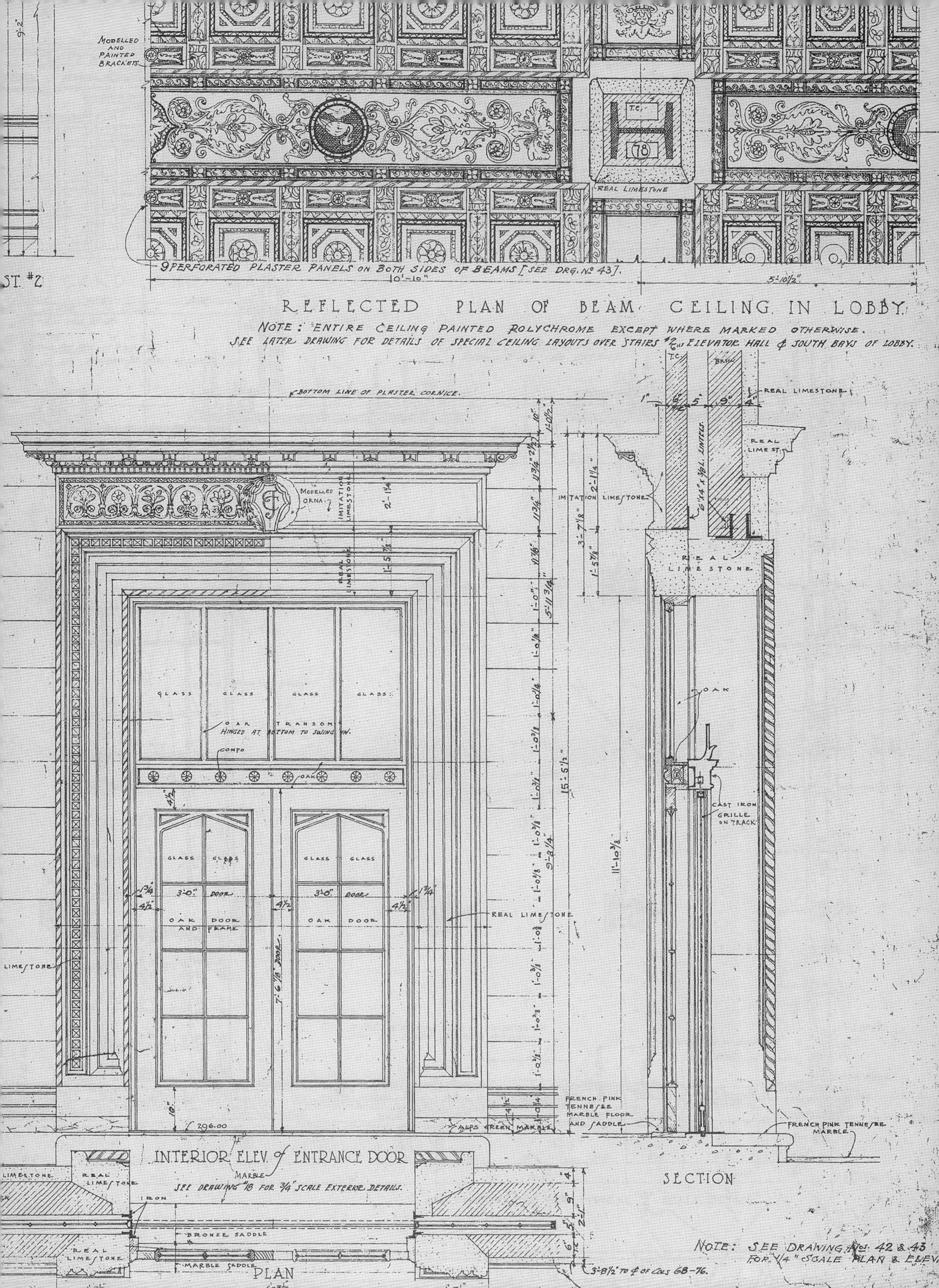

THE BELLEVUE TERRACE HOTEL
WAS HERE FIRST

The fashionable Bellevue Terrace Hotel was on the corner of Sixth and Figueroa Streets before The Jonathan Club was. In fact, the Bellevue Terrace Hotel was here before there was even a full intersection of Sixth and Figueroa, and even before there was a Figueroa Street. Figueroa was called Pearl Street and Sixth Street deadended at Pearl. The hotel was at the far limit of the horse-drawn rail car.

The Bellevue Terrace advertised rooms for $30 a month and up, for a single occupant and $55 if two people occupied the room. The hotel featured a pool room and weekly card parties and dancing events. Helen Hunt Jackson sat at the Bellevue Terrace and wrote her famous novel "Ramona," about the badly abused Indians of the Southwest.

An 1892 ad for the hotel read:

> *Where are you going to stop whilst in Los Angeles? Why at the Bellevue Terrace Hotel. It is the only first-class family house in the city where you can get large sunny rooms, with free baths and good attention, broad porches, beautiful lawns and table the best on the Coast, at living prices. Hotel corner of Sixth and Pearl Streets.*

Sixth Street ran west from what was then the city's core along Spring and Main Streets, but it ended at Pearl Street (later renamed Figueroa) with little more than a foot path continuing west. Bellevue Terrace was a suburban hotel, well away from downtown Los Angeles.

By the time Jeffries and his board entered into a lease for the property the Bellevue Terrace had already been razed and a parking lot occupied the corner.

Today the upscale gift shop of the Jonathan Club is named Bellevue Terrace in honor of the prestigious hotel that once stood there.

A prestigious address: Grasshopper Street

The Jonathan Club's street was originally Calle de los Chapules, or Grasshopper Street. In 1849, it was a short, muddy street that ended near where the Jonathan Club is today. Grasshopper Street became Pearl Street. In the mid-1800s a number of streets were renamed for the eleven governors of Alta California, who reined from 1822 to 1846. The sixth of these, and most able, was Brevet-Brigadier General José Secundino Figueroa y Parra. After that the street which is now Figueroa was named Figueroa south of Pico and Pearl Street north of Pico. The street we now know as Boylston took up the name of Figueroa at Sixth Street and kept the Figueroa name as it continued north. This confusion was corrected around the turn of the twentieth century, when the name Figueroa was applied to the entire length of the street which bears its name today.

Here we see the intersection of Figueroa and Sixth Streets around 1898. The stone wall in the lower right corner is the southeastern edge of the Bellevue Terrace Hotel Property (where the Town Club is today). Sixth Street appears as little more than a dusty trail as it continues west past Figueroa.

A lithograph of an unknown artist looking south down Pearl Street (Figueroa) from the top of the Bellevue Terrace Hotel in 1885. This perspective is from what would today be the Fourth Floor of the Jonathan Club. Portions of the Bellevue Terrace Hotel itself are part of the foreground.

This photograph taken in 1916 shows the west side of Figueroa between Sixth and Fifth Streets. A portion of the Bellevue Terrace Hotel (where the Town Club stands today) is visible in the lower left corner. The intersection with Fifth Street is visible at the right edge of the photo.

In 1946, Figueroa Street was famous because its intersection with Sunset Boulevard was labeled the busiest in vehicular traffic in the world. Today, Figueroa Street stretches from Eagle Rock to Wilmington, a distance of nearly 30 miles. The portion of Figueroa where the Jonathan Club is located today was a residential district of large homes at the turn of the 20th century.

SIXTH AND FIGUEROA
BECOMES HOME

Just as it had twenty years earlier, The Jonathan Club wowed Southern California with the magnificence of its new quarters. This was the fourth home for The Jonathan Club but the first in its very own building. There was so much to celebrate that the membership had to be split into two separate opening events.

The new Italian Renaissance building was so impressive that the California Club was finally inspired to build its own new quarters. The prestigious English Automobile Club studied plans of clubs throughout the world in preparation for its own new facility in England and rated the new Jonathan Club the finest. The Club quarters were built to the 150-foot height limit of the time. Until 1957, only the Los Angeles City Hall had been allowed greater height.

The $3 million building was opened officially on December 14, 1925, with a membership dinner in the Main Dining Room and the Game (Grill) Room attended by 600 members. Two other opening dinners followed within a week, the first of which included wives and the second of which included guests. Twenty-three of the original members were alive at the time and 15 attended the opening ceremony.

Today, the visitor is most struck with the ornate Italian Renaissance craftsmanship that hints of European palaces. Yet in its day its awe came from its vast amount of automobile parking space. The automobile had been unknown on Los Angeles streets when the Club was established, in 1895, and was still a novelty when the Club moved into the Pacific Electric Building, in 1905. Now, in 1925, society had all but abandoned horse-drawn transportation in favor of trolleys and automobiles. The high water mark for trolley travel in the U. S. had been reached in 1922, with the automobile becoming more dominant every year thereafter.

The Jonathan Club headquarters was a building which catered to the full range of club benefits. It contained breathtaking spaces for large events, rooms for games and a 10-chair barber shop off the Lobby. While the Club emphasized that it was "in no sense ... an athletic club" its "gymnasium and plunge" were impressive nevertheless. According to the *Los Angeles Evening Herald*, "the new building is said to be the first social club of the west to incorporate all the features of an athletic club into its home."

Half of the floors were set aside for the building's 250 overnight rooms, so that the Club functioned much like a hotel. Its Lobby served guests with a large front desk of barred windows and with a large counter for cigars, candy and newspapers.

The ground level south of the front door was retail space. The retail spaces at 547 and 549 South Figueroa were leased to Myron F. Schilling for a floral shop. There has been a flower shop in the Club almost continually since the building opened. The space at the corner of Sixth and Figueroa was leased to Harry A. Dutton as a drug store. He wanted to name it "Jonathan Drug Company" but the board deemed this "inadvisable."

The club offices were on the Sixth Floor. The top floor was called a Solarium, with grass carpets and wicker furniture. It was off limits to all but Jonathan Club members.

The Jonathan Town Club was built before the age of television, of course, but also before the age of popular radio. Commercial radio had just been established a few years earlier in 1922. The Jonathan Club was a gigantic game emporium. The Second Floor featured a large room for pool and billiards and another room for cards, dice, dominoes and board games. Members gathered in The Lounge on the third floor for games and in the Solarium on the roof for games. After men worked out on the Fifth Floor they cooled off with card games. Cigarette lighters were provided at tables with floor smokers for the ashes and occasional spittoons.

The Club squeezed every cent it had to build the luxurious Town Club in 1925. A grateful membership wanted to commission a portrait of William Jeffries for his leadership, but had no money. So each member of the Club was dunned two dollars, and Neale Ordayne painted the portrait. Ordayne was a portraitist from Chicago who lived in Los Angeles from 1925 till 1940.

WILLIAM PARRISH JEFFRIES

President in the best of times and the worst of times

The present character of the Jonathan Club owes more to William P. Jeffries than to any other figure. Ferd Rule fanned the initial ember and turned it into a lasting flame, but little of the nature of that 19th century men's club exsits in the 21st. Henry E. Huntington was the Club's president for 12 years and made two floors of his prestigious building available to the Club, but Huntington suggested no lasting innovations. On the other hand, Bill Jeffries inspired a Town Club facility that still defines the Club's physical culture 80 years later, and it was the same Bill Jeffries who led the Club to add a beach facility to its membership privileges. Thus, both the Town Club and the beach presence of the Jonathan Club owe homage to this visionary.

William Jeffries was an immensely self-confident figure who dreamed and acted on a giant plane. He burst onto the stage of Jonathan Club leadership and began to shape its destiny within days. Leaving behind a trail of directors who resigned their posts, he knew no pace other than flank speed. He painted history on an oversized canvas. In the end it was this very optimism and the dreaming of big dreams that was his undoing in The Jonathan Club.

William P. Jeffries was born November 8, 1908, in Mt. Sterling, Kentucky, but was educated in public schools in Los Angeles. He was assistant city engineer for Los Angeles in his early twenties, then formed the F. B. Kitts & Co. printing and engraving company, in 1894. In 1929, after a series of iterations, the firm had become the Jeffries Banknote Company. Jeffries was a member of the board of directors of a wide range of Southern California real estate, utility, banking, insurance and non-profit organizations.

He had joined The Jonathan Club in 1903, a year after Henry Huntington. He was elected to the board in 1923 and within minutes was chosen by that board to be the Club's president.

The Club had already decided to move from the Pacific Electric Building and had already targeted the vicinity of the current Town Club, but Jeffries turned that decision into immediate action. Jeffries' own initial vision for the new club was a facility costing about $750,000. By the day of its dedication he had dreamed the club into a palace costing $3 million. He grew the Club from two floors to 13 and doubled its membership from 1,000 members to 2,200 in a period of two years.

Jeffries was a creature of the sunshine of the 1920s, and his temperament was ill-suited for the storms and darkness of the 1930s. With the Depression already turning lights out all around, and with the staggering debt of the new Town Club, Jeffries committed the Club to a second facility, a huge club on the Santa Monica beach. The added debt was for a facility 60 percent as large as the Town Club, with 144 overnight rooms to be filled in a seasonal environment.

The board watched the impending financial collapse of the Club with such horror that it formed a "Member's Committee" whose assignment was to recommend changes to the leadership. The committee suggested that Jeffries and the Club treasurer needed to step down, and the two men did so. To show its respect for Jeffries, though, the board elected him "President Emeritus of The Jonathan Club," and he remained active in the Club's activities until his sudden death on June 12, 1935.

William Parrish Jeffries remains the most significant single individual in the Club's history. Even though he was asked to step down so that governance could switch to survival instead of more growth the Club continued to respect and admire this legendary leader. There is nothing in Club records to hint of any suspicion of personal gain in any of his actions. His large portrait hangs with honor in today's clubhouse and one of the Town Club's meeting rooms proudly bears his name. His grandson, Thomas L. Jeffries, led the Club as its president in 1983-84 and a great-grandson, William T. Jeffries, is an active Junior Member in Club today.

SUPPLIERS TO THE JONATHAN CLUB 1925

(The Club had committed itself to use "locally manufactured materials … as far as possible")

Architects: Schultze and Weaver
General Contractors: Lange & Bergstrom, Inc.
Boiler Brick Setting: Farris & Jones
Painting Contractors: Arenz-Warren Co., Inc.
Armstrong's Linotile: Van Fleet-Freear, Inc.
Asbestos Pipe Convering: Warren & Bailey Co.
Boilers: Llewellyn Iron Works
Cabinet Work: Commercial Fixture Co.
Composition Stairways and Floors: Diato Flooring Co.
Doors and Interior Woodwork: So. Cal. Hardwood & Mfg. Co.
Face Brick and Fire Brick: L. A. Pressed Brick Co.
Granite and Limestone: The McGilvray-Raymond Granite Co.
Hardwood Lumber: Nickey Bros., Inc.
Heating and Ventilating: Westinghouse Electric & Mfg. Co.
Hollow Metal Elevator Doors and Fronts: A. J. Bayer Co.
Hollow Tile: L.A. Pressed Brick Co.
Lime: Nevada Lime & Rock Corporation
Lumber: Hammond Lumber Co.
Ornamental Iron and Bronze: A. J. Bayer Co.
Ranges: Madsen Iron Works
Roof Tile: L. A. Pressed Brick Co.
Structural Steel Erected: Llewellyn Iron Works
Terra Cotta: Gladding, McBean & Co.
"Tuec" Vacuum Cleaning System: The United Electric Co.
Piano: Chickering

William P. Jeffries breaks ground for the Town Club. The second Mortgage Bonds were sold to members known as Red Star Men, hence the large red star at the groundbreaking. It is fitting that Jeffries wields the shovel alone, because the Jonathan Town Club was a reflection of his leadership, vision and energy. Architect Fullerton Weaver (light colored suit and vest) stands beside him. Weaver had presented Jeffries with the gold shovel, which was engraved:

> "Presented to William Parrish Jeffries, President of the Jonathan Club by Leonard Schultze and S. Fullerton Weaver as a token of appreciation and esteem for having accomplished the stupendous task of making the dream of a new Jonathan Club House a brilliant reality. The shovel is mightier than the pen or sword. Ground broken by William Parrish Jeffries, Monday, August 4, 1924."

SCHULTZE AND WEAVER

Premier architects for a premier club

On November 15, 1923, The Jonathan Club selected one of the most distinguished firms in the country to design its new facility, Schultze and Weaver of New York. The firm was headed by Leonard Schultze, an architect, and Spencer Fullerton Weaver, a civil engineer. Partnerships of architects and engineers are famous for pairing the creative with the down-to-earth, and that was true in this case. The surprise is that it was the engineer Weaver who was the creative soul and architect Schultze who was the pragmatist. According to Margaret L. Davis in her book "The Los Angeles Biltmore," Schultze was the hard-headed, practical architect" with a talent for conceiving a "project's overall design." He was "a perfectionist" and "a stickler for details and numbers." Weaver, on the other hand, "was more the dreamer and idealist…a plan's artistic genius."

The perfection of the elevator allowed Schultze and Weaver to create much of the spellbinding skyline above Manhattan during the 1920s and early 1930s. In his later years Schultze was not entirely happy with the urban form he had created. "New York was an attractive city before we started to develop it," he later said in a 1951 *New York Times* article.

Schultze was the senior partner, Weaver the junior. Among the architects who worked at the firm were Edward Durell Stone and Lawrence Murray Dixon.

S. Fullerton Weaver earned his degree in civil engineering from the University of Pennsylvania, in 1902. He served in France in World War I. Weaver was responsible for much of the development of Park Avenue in New York. He not only designed apartment buildings, but owned and managed some as well.

Leonard Schultze was born in Chicago and studied at the architectural school of the Metropolitan Museum of Art and under E. L. Masqueray. He served as a sergeant in the Spanish American War and during World War II he served as a consultant on the Board of War Engineers, North Atlantic Division. In 1903, only three years after entering the profession, he was made the chief of design for Grand Central Terminal. During his life Schultze designed hotels, hospitals, homes, multi-family complexes and private clubs. He died in 1951, at the age of 73, in a hospital he had designed. The firm of Schultze and Weaver was especially distinguished in creating landmark hotels, and the Jonathan Town Club has many hotel-like characteristics. In fact, when the rival California Club built its own facility in 1930 it went to great pains to avoid "hotel type" design, an obvious reference to the new Jonathan Club.

Opposite: Artist Lloyd Morgan (1892-1970) created an oil painting of an imaginary city composed entirely of buildings designed by Schultze and Weaver between 1921 and 1936. The painting was lost, but fortunately a photograph of the painting survives. The three tallest buildings, left to right, are Hotel Pierre, the Waldorf-Astoria Hotel and the Sherry Netherland Hotel.

The stock market crash of 1929 killed the market for grand, ornate hotels. Fullerton Weaver died in 1939, before the country had emerged from the Depression. Schultze renamed his firm Leonard Schultze & Associates and, after World War II, used his genius for organizing large projects to design huge, practical multi-family complexes. Some of these were financed by Metropolitan Life Insurance Company.

At the time the firm was designing The Jonathan Club, Schultze and Weaver had offices at the Pacific Mutual Building, 523 West Sixth Street. In late 1923, both Schultze and Weaver had made Los Angeles their permanent homes and both joined The Jonathan Club. Both left The Jonathan Club after the stock market crash and moved back to New York.

BUILDINGS DESIGNED BY LEONARD SCHULTZE AND FULLERTON WEAVER:

Shultze and Weaver

Waldorf-Astoria Hotel (6)
New York, 47 stories, 1931

Hotel Pierre Hotel (9)
New York, 41 stories, 1930

Hotel Sherry Netherland
New York, 40 stories, 1927

Barbizon Plaza Hotel
New York, 40 stories, 1930

Hotel Lexington
New York, 28 stories, 1928

Clift Hotel (7)
San Francisco, 15 stories, 1926

Ingraham Building
Miami, 13 stories, 1927

Hunter-Dulin Building
San Francisco, 22 stories, 1926

Biltmore Hotel
Coral Gables, 15 stories, 1926

Biltmore Hotel
Los Angeles, 11 stories, 1923

Roney-Plaza Hotel (2)
Miami Beach, 17 stories, 1925

Atlanta Biltmore Hotel
Atlanta, 11 stories, 1924

Sevilla Biltmore Hotel
Havana, Cuba

Subway Terminal Building
Los Angeles, 12 stories, 1925

Freedom Tower (Miami News)
Miami, 17 stories, 1925

Hellman Commerical Trust and Savings Bank Building
Los Angeles, 1924

Breakers Hotel (3)
Palm Beach, 8 stories, 1925

Leonard Schultze (with other firms)
Grand Central Terminal (1)
New York, 1913

Biltmore Hotel (4)
New York

Commodore Hotel
New York

Ambassador Hotel (5)
New York

New York Central Headquarters
New York

Leonard Schultze and Archibald Manning Brown
Heinz Dome food pavilion
New York World's Fair, 1937

Leonard Schultze and Associates
640 5th Ave.
New York, 20 stories, 1949

15 E. 91st St.
New York, 17 stories, 1948

Park La Brea Apartments (8)
Los Angeles, 1942

47 E. 87th St.
New York, 16 stories, 1947

Parkfairfax
Virginia, 1941-1943

(Numbers in parenthases refer to post card images on pages 58-59)

*Buildings designed by Schultze and Weaver or by Leonard Schultze.
Refer to numbered list on previous page for building names.*

Opposite: The Town Club in the late 1940s before the Harbor Parkway (Freeway) and off-ramp were built. Note the forest of vegetation above the Fifth Floor.

Above: Over the years, the Town Club has not changed much, but there have been changes. Note the two-story garage added to the north side of the building in 1953.

Below: Two additional floors were added to the garage in 1970. This photograph was taken while the Atlantic Richfield Towers were being constructed.

In 1958, the street appearance of the Town Club was "refreshed and updated" by filling in the "dated" arches with terracotta brick. Club member Earl T. Heitschmidt, of Heitschmidt and Thompson architects, designed the facade. Club president Ralph E. Fife said at the time, "we don't do things today the way we did in 1925." Apparently the design community agreed with Fife, because the Southern California Chapter of the American Institute of Architects bestowed its Fine Craftsman Award on Koegh Bros., the firm that executed the masonary of the facade. Some older members today say that the brick facades were installed for security because the neighborhood around the Town Club had deteriorated.

The Town Club's front entrance has changed again and again over the years. Originally there was a slight step up at the front door. Terrazzo was installed at a slope, perhaps in the 1940s, eliminating the step. Revolving doors were installed in 1926 and removed in 1947.

GIOVANNI BATTISTA SMERALDI

The artsian who made the Town Club special

Giovanni Battista Smeraldi was one of the foremost Italian artisans of his day. Trained on the ceilings of the Vatican, he moved to the United States and went by the prosaic name of John D. Smeraldi. It is Smeraldi's work that is so admired on the ceilings of the Jonathan Town Club.

Smeraldi painted the ceilings of Caltech's Athenaeum, New York's Grand Central Terminal and the Blue Room of the White House. Smeraldi was also the artisan for the Biltmore Hotel in Los Angeles. His legacy is so great at that hotel that its restaurant has been renamed in his honor: Smeraldi's.

Among his commissions were several Vanderbilt houses, the Biltmore Hotels in Atlanta and Miami, the Breakers Hotel in Palm Beach, the Chateau Frontenac in Quebec, the Pacific-Southwest Trust and Savings Bank in Pasadena, the Security Bank in Long Beach, the Hellman Bank in Los Angeles and the Hall of Justice in Los Angeles. He was summoned to Canada, Cuba and Puerto Rico to execute his art.

Among his apprentices was A. T. Heinsbergen. Heinsbergen became Smeraldi's biggest competitor in Southern California. Years later Heinsbergen restored the Smeraldi ceilings of both the Jonathan Club and the Biltmore Hotel.

Giovanni Battista Smeraldi was born in Palermo, Italy, in 1867 and educated in Rome. He came to the United States in 1889. His specialty was the European Renaissance style of architectural decoration, a style much in favor during the 1920s. He was also known as a furniture designer. A Pasadena resident, he came to California in 1923. He died at age 79, in 1947.

*Ceilings of the Town Club Lobby (upper photo),
Main Dining Room (lower left) and Grill Room (lower right)*

Chapter 4
Town Club Spaces

In 1925, the Lobby was much busier than it is today. The main desk, with its bank-teller bars, is visible on the left in the top photo, and the cigar stand can be seen on the right.

THE LOBBY

A grand entrance

The Lobby of the Jonathan Town Club has changed much since members first created a human pulse in 1925. There was probably much more traffic on its floors in the 1920s. The front desk operation was in the lobby itself, along the wall where guests now find coffee service in the mornings and sherry in the evening. The desk had bars over its several windows, looking much like bank counters of its day. The present telephone/computer room was the office of the desk manager. The area where the club desk sits today, across from the elevators, was a large check room.

On the other side of the entryway to the elevators and stairway, where the concierge desk sits today, was a large cigar counter, where cigarettes, candy and newspapers were also sold. The longest tenured employee in the Club's history, Jane Lauman, began her career as a "cigarette girl" at this counter in 1940, and retired from the Club in 2005, 65 years later, after having served in a number of departments. In the southwest corner of the lobby was the door to the 10-chair barber shop. Today there is no entry to the barber shop from the Lobby.

A non-working fireplace of 1925 was taken out years ago, then another fireplace eventually was installed at the same location, but it is quite different in appearance.

French Pink Tennessee marble covered the floors, set off by dark Alps Green marble. The carpet in the lobby on opening day measured 35x78 feet and weighed 8,700 pounds.

A mezzanine added a half story to the room all along its northern side, and was contained in the space between the columns and the northern wall. That northern wall of today's Lobby was the outside wall of the building in the beginning, and there were windows to the outside where the mirror "windows" are today. A skirt of doors with curtains hiding glass panes divided the lobby from the walkway beneath the mezzanine, creating a buffer to the lobby itself for those who arrived by automobile. The auto driveway ran along the northern side of the Jonathan Club, immediately on the other side of the wall that forms the northern side of the Lobby today.

Women arriving at the Club were not allowed in the Main Lobby. At the eastern end of the hallway beneath the mezzanine was a small "Ladies' Elevator." Women arriving by automobile arrived at the Entrance Vestibule's west end and proceeded directly to their own elevator. For women arriving by trolley or on foot after shopping on Seventh Avenue there a separate "Ladies' Entrance" from Figueroa, which brought women directly to the "Ladies' Waiting Room."

The mezzanine was used in later years for a ticket broker desk and a public stenographer. Originally it was simply an extension of the main lobby and was furnished as "a veritable museum of rare Chinese art objects."

By the 1940s, a small square booth had replaced the cigar stand. In that booth sat an attendant who checked the membership of those entering.

During the Depression and World War II the Lobby suffered from wear and tear and lack of funds for upkeep. The large marble sculpture of Greek wrestlers that had adorned the Jonathan Club lobby in the Pacific Electric Building prolonged their frozen combat in the Town Club lobby in the 1940s. In 1925, the sculpture had been placed in the Reading Room. The Lobby was refreshed in 1955 when the fireplace was replaced with wallpaper and an oversized Jonathan Club logo. Furniture that only the 1950s could love was moved in.

In 1958, one member complained to the board of directors:

"Gentlemen: The lobby is getting to look like the Ghetto. One loud voiced woman sounds like a fog horn. Last night I looked up and saw a fat man with a red jersey. These things look good on Maxwell Street Chicago. One cannot carry a conversation in lobby due to these distractions. Please do something in keeping with the fine standards of our wonderful Club."

But it was what happened to the Lobby in 1970 that serves as one of the most discouraging elements of Jonathan Club history to some of its current members. The original 1925 lobby was effectively destroyed in the name of progress. The 1969 board of directors was tired of the "dated" Italian Renaissance craftsmanship that had held such appeal for an earlier generation. It hired the interior design firm of Cannell & Chaffin to give it "an aura of elegance, simplicity and masculinity."

The 1970 board stripped away the elegant dark wood wainscoting, hammered wood panels onto walls and over the stone columns, laid wall-to-wall carpeting over the marble floor and dismantled the mezzanine. It replaced the 1925 chandeliers with fixtures "simple in design and having a natural wood spindle effect," emitting "a warm glow and sparkle through globes of amber crackled glass." The front desk in the lobby was "updated" as well and the check-in booth was sold to a Club member who installed it in his basement as a bar.

In 1981, much of the damage of the 1970 design was undone, through the direction of architect Peter Kudrave and interior designer Logan Brown. The wall-to-wall carpeting was removed, along with the 1970 furniture. The monstrous crackled-glass chandeliers were also replaced and some of the original furnishings were brought back. At this time the front desk was no longer the "bank cage" original, but was a long simple counter. Two desks and two staffs were being maintained, one in the lobby, the other in front of the elevators where coats could be left and hats checked in large pigeon-hole bins. In 1981, the desk by the elevators took on front desk duties and the lobby front desk function was eliminated entirely, freeing the Club's waiting room from the hubbub of business dealings. The check-in booth was given back to the Club by the member who'd bought it in 1970. The booth now sits by the entrance to the flower shop.

When the wall-to-wall carpeting was removed a wooden floor was discovered in the Ladies Lobby under the mezzanine. Then with the mezzanine and the wall-to-wall carpeting gone, the marble floor did not extend across the lobby. Logan Brown knew that similar marble had been used by I. M. Pei in the National Gallery in Washington. He was able to order French Pink Tennessee marble from the same quarry that had produced the original 1925 flooring. It almost defies the current visitor to find the boundary between the 1925 and the 1981 installations.

In 1982, the ceilings of Giovanni Battista Smeraldi were repainted by A. T. Heinsbergen and Company, the firm that had recently restored the California State Capitol in Sacramento. A. T. Heinsbergen had learned his craft from Smeraldi, and had broken away in 1922 to become Smeraldi's major competitor. In 1982, the firm was headed by A. T.'s son, Tony Heinsbergen. The Heinsbergen crew members photographed the original ceiling artwork, tracing the design and matching the colors. They then scraped off the badly flaking parts and applied a base coat of new paint. Then the gilt areas were redone. Then the entire ceiling was overglazed with a continuous coat of translucent paint and wiped to create a stippled effect.

The board had a limited budget for the rehabilitation of the Lobby, so it approved draperies to hide the neglected north wall. Those draperies stayed in place until 2000, when the Club finally finished the restoration. The Lobby wall was restored for fine art and mirrored window forms were installed as hints that this wall, now separating the Lobby from the Garage, was once the outside wall of the Club and did, indeed, have windows.

The original Lobby included a mezzanine along the north wall. The center photo on the bottom shows one of the many Lobby facelifts.

The mezzanine along the north wall of the Lobby was removed in 1970.

The cigar counter stood on the south side of the Lobby where the concierge desk stands today. The Lobby was built in 1925 with a door directly to the Barber Shop.

The Elevator Story

There were no elevators in the two Jonathan Club locations on Spring Street, but elevators played a large role in the Club culture at the Pacific Electric Building. The Club sat on the eighth and ninth floors and was reached by two elevators dedicated to The Jonathan Club. Women rode up the elevator with men to the seventh floor, but had to walk up a distant stairway to reach the next floor where The Jonathan Club began. Over the 20 years at the Pacific Electric Building, women began riding up to the club itself with their husbands, and this caused such a problem that the Town Club at Sixth and Figueroa Streets was designed with a solution to this common complaint. A separate elevator would be installed to carry women in their own shaft, unseen by men in the Club's main elevators.

No sooner had the new club opened when some members began to complain about this arrangement, demanding to ride with their wives on elevators in the Club. Husbands and wives traveled together to a Jonathan Club gala and entered the building together. But husband and wife rode their separate elevators to the third floor, where they were reunited. The voices protesting this system continued over the years but they were in the minority. Minutes of a 1959 Public Relations Committee asked, "Why can't men accompany their women guests to the third floor by using the same elevator?…some women coming into the main lobby flutter around like a chicken in a strange barnyard, so confused are they in locating the proper elevator." Women and men made their way up and down in separate lifts until 1971, when House Rule 14 was changed "to permit gentlemen to accompany their ladies and guests in the Ladies' Elevator." In 1974, women were finally permitted in the Club's main elevators.

The three main elevators built with the building, for men only, were cable hoists running at 600 feet per minute. The Ladies Elevator was a hydraulic machine operating at half that speed. There were also two service elevators.

All elevators were originally operated by attendants. In 1966-67, in a process that took the better part of a year, the cabs of the three main elevators were replaced and the elevators were automated, "following the practice now in vogue in many hotels, office buildings and hospitals," according to minutes of the board, in 1962. The

Today's main desk facing the elevators was once the hat check desk.

Club didn't quite go cold turkey, though. An attendant was still employed as an elevator starter. About the same time, the Club's paging system was piped into the cabs.

In 1964, the board pondered the future possibility of women on the thirteenth floor, and thus considered installing an escalator between the twelfth and thirteenth floors.

The Ladies' Elevator was finally automated in 1970. It finished out the 20th century offering a shortcut for women to their Sixth Floor sports and fitness locker room. When luxury suites were installed, in 2003, the modification to the eighth and ninth floors penetrated the shaft of Ladies' Elevator, and the cab was taken down to the Lobby level and deactivated, turning a page of Jonathan Club history.

The décor of the main elevator cabs has been changed repeatedly over the years, variously displaying wood paneling, wood forms, fabric and mirrors. The metal elevator doors on the fifth floor were installed in 1996.

In 1956, the original barber chairs were replaced with the chairs that still serve the shop today.

THE BARBER SHOP

In 1914, while in the Pacific Electric Building, the board authorized the "purchase of linoleum, a mirror and 'other proper equipment' for a barber shop and two years later, in 1916, enough hair was being cut to authorize a second barber, to work on a commission basis. The second chair was to be rented for two months before committing to a purchase. A month later the Club hired its first "Manicurist for gentlemen and ladies" and a month after that a bootblack was added.

In 1956 the classic barber chairs of the 1920s were replaced with chairs of the time and those 1956 chairs are still in use at the Town Club today. Mudpack facials were offered in the 1950s. In boom days of 1960 the number of manicurists was increased from three to four. Today the barber shop is served by three barbers, a manicurist and a shoe shine attendant.

In 1935 the Club offered The Golden System Scalp Treatment to grow hair. The hair-growing system involved "scientific manipulation of the nerve and circulatory centers of the shoulders, neck and scalp," and was overseen by the system's originators, Mr. and Mrs. R.A. Finch. The offering was short lived.

The Bellevue Terrace gift shop, just off the Lobby, is named for the hotel that stood at Sixth and Figueroa Streets prior to the Town Club's construction. The shop is in the addition built in 1953.

The Town Club has been served by a number of gift shops in various locations over the years. Pictured left is the gift shop of 1937.

The Town Club Garage

Today's visitor to the Town Club marvels at its Italian Renaissance décor and ornate public rooms, but one of the most impressive features at the 1925 Club debut was its garage. The Club's 1924 roster cooed, "The *outstanding feature* in the New Home, in the opinion of some of its members, will lie just apart from the Club, in the Garage!" The *Los Angeles Examiner* said, "In the estimation of Mr. Jeffries, one of the most successful features of the new club is a…garage." An early brochure said, "A capacious Lounge has been designed for your chauffeurs, with electric connections and announcers to summon them when wanted." Many automobiles of that day were electric and charging stations were provided.

The original automobile entrance was on Sixth Street, which was at that time simply a street, not a freeway off-ramp. A narrow covered driveway ran the length of north side of the building, emptying onto Figueroa. The original garage held 450 automobiles. In 1953 the Club surveyed its members on whether to build a parking structure onto the north side of the building. A total of 1,801 said yes and only 72 were opposed. The Club bought a vacant parking lot to its north and two small parcels to the northwest and southwest of the Town Club to fill out its occupation of the entire southern half of the block and in 1953 built an addition to its garage, upping its capacity to 750 cars.

Jonathan Club member Earl Heitschmidt, who acted as the Club's architect on many improvements, along with member Whiting Thompson, was the project architect. P. J. Walker Co. was the contractor. Heitschmidt and Thompson created a contemporary façade that they felt complemented the original building's design. Later generations would shake their heads at the design sense of the 1950s that created an appearance that in later times would be viewed as a jarring insult to the original design. It must be remembered, though, that 1953 was less than 30 years after the building was built. Do we, today, view with religious respect the building elements of the late 1970s and consider them inviolate in our rehabilitations?

Previous page: Originally there were two entrances and exits to the garage, one off Sixth Street (before it was a freeway off ramp) and the other off Figueroa Street, which was a two-way thoroughfare at the time. The present garage entrance was not built until 1953, so for the first 28 years, cars entered from Figueroa through this porte-cochere. The main entryway under the porte-cochere was where the north Lobby doors are today.

The Library
The Town Club's inviolate sanctuary

The Library consists of two reading rooms, and always has. The large Reading Room is to the east and the library itself is to the west. Windows lined the north wall, both in the Reading Room and in the stacks, until the garage addition covered them up.

It is almost a miracle that the Town Club's Library has survived the mania for "improvement" and re-designation that has plagued other public spaces in the building. It has never been wood-paneled or drop-ceilinged and has never been carved up for other uses. It remains the quiet sanctuary for reading and reflection that it was in 1925. Yet in every member generation it occurs to someone that the Library is "wasted space," a place that is often unoccupied, a prime candidate for a banquet hall, room for card players, entryway to the Club or worse.

Just as New York's Central Park has withstood the temptations of development in a city starved for space, the Jonathan Town Club's Library has been protected as a large, open, elegant space. Sitting in the Library one witnesses a procession of members showing guests "their" Library, with obvious pride. Certainly that much space is not needed for the function, just as the Lobby could function with far less space and far lower ceilings.

The Jonathan Club has included a reading room since at least 1896 at its 132 South Spring Street location. An elegant Reading Room was built into the 1905 Pacific Electric Building space, and its function as a library grew from its first year. An initial $500 for book purchases was voted by the board in 1905 and Club President Henry Huntington found a library that the Club purchased for $3,500.

In 1934, the Library was considered as a site for card players, if their current room behind the Grill Room became "too crowded." In 1966, the board seriously considered taking 1,000 square feet out of the Reading Room for a second floor entrance from the parking structure into the Club.

A small, dusty mineral collection is displayed in a special cabinet in the Library stacks. This is perhaps the collection, or the remnants of one, accepted by the Club in its brand new Pacific Electric Building headquarters in 1905, and displayed there in a specially-built cabinet.

Except for the furnishings, the Library looks much as it did in 1925, with a large Reading Room and separate library section. Today, just as it was in 1925, the entrance to the stacks is guarded by two cloisonné black urns that came over from the old building. Before the garage was heightened in 1970, there were windows along the north wall in the Reading Room and in the library alcoves. The "lounging rooms" on either side of the fireplace were created in 1926. Four learned faces look down from the 1925 library "woodwork": Shakespeare, Cicero, Dante and Hippocrates.

About 2,000 volumes were brought from the old headquarters in 1925, and by 1939 the library boasted between 3,000 to 4,000 books, despite a slim budget. (The Library's new book budget in 1940 was $5 a month.) Today's library contains between 6,000 to 7,000 volumes.

All that's missing at the far end of the Library is a crackling fire. Alas, this was never a functioning fireplace. Four cultural sentinels watch over the stacks in the Library: Hippocrates, Shakespeare, Cicero and Dante.

From Billiard Room to Tap Room

The Tap Room was originally a Billiard Room with eight pool tables and four billiard tables. There was no bar at all. This was during Prohibition.

Two gargoyle figures are repeated throughout the room. One holds a pool cue; the other keeps score. Colorful tile wainscoting, designed by Jonathan Earl Heitschmidt and fired by Gladding, McBean & Co., was intended to reflect local craftsmanship. The overhead beams were painted by Giovanni Smeraldi, who also designed the ceilings of the Lobby, Florentine Lounge and Main Dining Room.

Famous pool, snooker and billiard players gave demonstrations here. In 1942, three of the billiard tables were converted to snooker, and about the same time air conditioning was installed.

In 1940, a Tap Room was opened in the space now occupied by the second floor men's restroom, but by the 1950s the thirst of the members overwhelmed this relatively small bar.

The Billiard Room, on the men-only second floor, was the obvious candidate. Drinkers debated pool players for years and the 1954 board of directors finally acted to replace cue sticks with swizzle sticks. For reassurance, the board surveyed the membership in a non-binding vote. The membership agreed with the board. The obstinate pool players used the Club's bylaws to call a general meeting, on October 6, 1954, for the membership to decide. The 400 members present settled the question once and for all: Bar space was carved out of the parking garage west of the Grill Room for a new Billiard Room and $82,660 was budgeted for converting the old Billiard Room to a drinking emporium.

The new drinking hall was completed on December 15, 1954. The hand-rubbed, black walnut bar, almost 50 feet long, was touted to be one of the longest bars in the United States. The Club's collection of beer steins was placed on a high shelf over the bar. The stein collection was probably started in 1905 in the bar of the new clubhouse at the Pacific Electric Building. Because there was no publicly known bar in the Town Club when it opened during Prohibition in 1925 the stein collection was displayed over the grill in the Game Room (now Grill Room). At least one of the steins now on display over the Tap Room bar dates back to the 1905 bar in the Pacific Electric Building. After the 1954 opening of the new Tap Room there had been over 100 objects of art; today only 18 remain over the bar. Nine new bronze chan-

deliers were patterned after "original candlelight of Colonial times." Grousing pool players called it the "Chandelier Room."

The Club could not come up with an appropriate name for its new tap room, so for the time being they simply called it the "Tap Room." The "temporary" name continues a half century later.

Today's older members recall crowds three deep all along that popular bar, with drinks passed over the heads of other imbibers. But by the 1980s and 1990s society had changed. The after-work drink was no longer *de rigueur* and the Jonathan Club was no longer a men's institution. The cavernous bar was often empty.

The room was re-energized in 1999 with a sports bar personality to bring excitement back to the room. Nine television sets with myriad channels were nested every few yards to mesmerize patrons, and photos (old, but not necessarily significant) were queued around the room. Greater intimacy was created by booths that bisected the great hall and with vestibules to mask comings and goings. A pool table was returned in homage to the room's original use. Weekend meals were shifted from the Thirteenth Floor to the Tap Room to centralize food service.

In 1999, booths were constructed in the center of the room to create two separate spaces, with two distinct sets of tables and chairs, so that the one large room wouldn't seem so vacant. After patronage picked up again, the controversial middle booths were removed in 2003.

Since 1925, this room's ceiling competed with the grandeur of those in the Lobby and Main Dining Room. Over the years the paint began to peel. In one of the building's most unfortunate design crimes, a board of directors voted to install acoustic tiles over the damaged recessed portions of Giovanni Smeraldi's art and in 1981, ordered his intricate designs on the ceiling beams painted over. Restoration of Smeraldi's Tap Room ceiling design still awaits board funding as of this writing.

Today's Tap Room once again has active use. The tile wainscoting along the west wall is the original 1925 treatment. The collection of beer steins traces back to the early days of the Town Club and was originally displayed over the service bar in the Grill Room.

To show its appreciation for the leadership of the 1974-75 Club president a special cocktail was renamed the "Roy Houghton."

Their time long past, a snooker table and two pool tables sit idle most of the time in today's Town Club Billiard Room. These tables were originally in the popular, crowded Billiard Room, a space that has been used as the Tap Room, since the drinkers' lobby overpowered the pool players' lobby in the Club in 1954. One of the original 1925 pool tables was recently returned to the Tap Room, paying tribute to that room's first use. This is at least the third set of billiard tables owned by the Club. The Jonathan Club first bought billiard and pool tables in August of 1894 at its original 130 South Spring clubhouse. (This was before it became a social club.) A handsome matching set of tables was installed at 132 South Spring in 1896 and the new set of three billiard and three pool tables bought for the Pacific Electric Building in 1905 were said to be the finest tables on the Pacific Coast. An entirely new set of eight pool and four billiard tables was bought for the Town Club in 1925. Six of the tables were moved in 1954 to the new billiard room location. Three remain there.

In 1999, the Tap Room was transformed from a quiet, seldom-used bar to a lively, energy-filled, sports-bar-type tavern. The room was divided into two similar, but separate, rooms by booths across the mid-section of the space so that the room would not look so empty. After Tap Room usage picked up the center booths were removed.

The remarkable beer steins that overlook the 50-foot bar were originally displayed over the grill of the Game Room (Grill Room).

The gargoyles looking down on today's Tap Room betray the original use of the space. One holds a pool cue with a pool ball; the other keeps score.

The original 1925 tile work of Gladding, McBean & Co. is visible along the west side of the Tap Room. It once formed a belt around the entire room, but much of it is hidden by cabinets and the bar area today.

Acoustic tiles were slapped over Giovanni Smeraldi's ceiling, probably in 1954 or 1955. In 1983, Smeraldi's decorative artwork on the beams themselves, after surviving for 58 years, was painted over. The Smeraldi ceiling of the Tap Room was one of the distinctive elements of the Town Club and its restoration needs to be a priority.

This major Second Floor room was originally the Game Room (sometimes called the Card Room), and had a grill at the west end. At one time it had a fireplace, and at another time a lunch counter replaced the 1925 grill. Today another grill stands in the same place as the original. The original chairs are still in the room, although the upholstery has changed.

From Game Room to Grill Room

The ornate room known today as the Grill Room was originally the Game Room. The room was filled with tables to accommodate four, five or six players at games of cards, chess, cribbage, dominoes and checkers.

The Game Room became known as the Second Floor Men's Grill, The Grill or Grille before settling into its present Grill Room name. The room was reserved for men only until 1989.

In 1925, a large grill formed a bow at the west end of the room, where a different grill is installed today. Behind the counter were a steam table and three prominent cabinets. Two of the cabinets were for pastry and salad. The largest of the three cabinets was reserved for tobacco. (Priorities were different in those days!) Beer steins lined a high shelf over the grill, perhaps the same ornate steins now on display in the Tap Room. Waiters brought snacks from the grill to those winning and losing at the tables.

The Town Club was built during Prohibition, yet the Grill Room was designed for the pining Jonathans like an English "taproom." Dark oak paneling was set off by a plaster ceiling that was stamped with sandblasted boards to give a natural wood appearance.

Over the years the room evolved from a game room with food service to a food service room with games and finally to a room devoted exclusively to food. On March 31, 1947, a separate space, named the Stag Game Room, opened immediately behind the Grill Room. Carved out of former parking space the new room offered Jonathans "more latitude in playing hours" and freed the Grill Room to concentrate on food service. The new game room had its own restroom and a staff attendant called "the game warden." Sheriff Gene Biscailuz, an active Jonathan, donated a collection of guns for display in the new game room. The game room is still in daily use, but over the years most of Sheriff Biscailuz's guns have mysteriously disappeared.

During the Depression the Grill Room was rented to the public as a banquet facility to help generate cash flow for the Club. This was stopped in 1938. During those tough years lunch in the Men's Grill cost 50 cents and men could expect to find the 11:30 edition of the *Los Angeles Herald-Express* for late news in days when "print journalism" was a redundancy. It was during the Depression that a long-lasting Grill Room tradition began. A "buffet carriage" with seafood was introduced in the Fall of 1936. The seafood trolley!

Gargoyles in the Grill Room originally watched a room full of men playing cards, dice, dominoes and board games. One gargoyle holds playing cards, one holds a dice cup and two others watch in amusement.

In the 1930s, a sit-down lunch counter was installed as an anteroom for Jonathans on the go. (The original grill had disappeared some years before.) In 1941, a fireplace was built at the west end of the room and later that year air conditioning was installed in the Grill Room. A grill was re-introduced at the west end in 1956.

The period of the late 40s through the early 70s was a time of great architectural mischief throughout the building, when the Italian Renaissance décor was no longer part of public taste and not yet old enough to be appreciated as historical. Rubber tile was installed as soon as wartime shortages abated. Acoustical tiles were glued over the wood stamped ceilings in the early 1950s. A supplement to *The Jonathan* magazine in 1950 said, "The ceiling of the second floor grille room should be sound-proofed to cut down the noise that is serious and annoying during the busy hours." The tiles were removed in the 1980s.

Today's Grill Room retains the pillars, gargoyles and ceilings that watched over the great grandfathers of today's members. The wood paneling is original, although it's been lightened from its original dark oak look. Today's Grill Room chairs are the original 1925 furniture, but are covered today in leather instead of their original patterned upholstery. The overhead lights are different, however.

In 1993, the room was broken up with booths and cubicles for the first time in its history. This configuration was inspired by the venerable Tadich Grill in San Francisco. The cubicles included telephones and space for papers on the table and each of the spaces had curtains to shield these violations of longstanding Club policy. The board at the time even saw the possibility of watching television for stock quotes while hidden by curtains. Though the curtains are seldom drawn today for their intended business purpose, once in a great while one might see waiters respecting the privacy of a couple until the occupants push the button inside the cubicle to turn on a discreet service light visible on the outside.

The caricatures of members on the wall today are by Orange County cartoonist Daniel Minamide, who draws under the name of "Dan the Cartoon Man," and were installed begining in 1993. Cartoons are not new to the Club. In 1916 the Club traded cartoonist E. E. McDowell a membership for his art and in 1938 a collection of cartoons of Club members drawn by H.G. Webster was displayed in the Library.

THE REAGAN ROOM

From a women's refuge to a shrine for great Americans

The Jonathan Club had a problem in the Pacific Electric Building, and it was determined to solve that problem in its new quarters at Sixth and Figueroa. The Pacific Electric Building was laid out in a way that made it difficult to keep the members-only facilities separate from those it shared with wives. The architect's solution in the new building was to provide a separate women's entrance off Figueroa (a door still visible off to the right through the iron grate at the entranceway), a separate women's lobby and a separate women's elevator to ferry women to the floors where they were allowed. The "Ladies' Department" was a suite of two large rooms on the third floor: a Ladies Lounge and Ladies Dining Room. Those two rooms are combined today in a public room named the Reagan Room. The Ladies' Elevator delivered women to what is now the northeast corner of the Reagan Room, offering "the Janets of the Jonathan Club" "their private service to the lounge, where they can wait in comfort for their male escorts and friends."

The Ladies Lounge was a large living room where women could gather, play cards, converse and relax between shopping forays to the department stores on Seventh Street or on other trips to downtown Los Angeles. This room was on the Figueroa Street side. The other end of today's Reagan Room was the Ladies Dining Room. The interior design and decoration of the two rooms were quite different. The windows that lined the north sides of both rooms were sealed off after the construction of the garage additions of the 1970.

These rooms devoted to women were redecorated more often than any other rooms in the building. Originally the walls of the lounge were covered in a "daintily figured satin cover" and the dining room was furnished in a Chippendale motif. In 1933, the Ladies Lounge was briefly the Parisienne Room "in step with the legal enactment of repeal." A year later the two rooms were redecorated by Vern Fiske of Longford Studios "to reflect the trend of the times...a smartly modern way," and the name of the dining room was changed to the Blue Room, and fitted with trendy Venetian blinds. The terms Blue Room and Ladies Dining Room were used interchangeably after that.

In 1955, the women's entrance off the main lobby, the Ladies' Elevator, the Ladies Lounge and the Ladies Dining Room were completely redecorated and air conditioned. In keeping with the "enlightenment" of the 1950s, a drop ceiling and acoustical tiles were installed, essentially

What is today one large space called the Reagan Room was originally two distinct rooms in the "Ladies Department." The Ladies Lounge was at the east end (top) and the Ladies Dining Room was on the west side (bottom).

Over the years, the two women's spaces were redecorated more than were any other public rooms in the club.

destroying the proud arches of the 1925 designs for the two rooms. The stone columns of the Lounge were covered with mirrors and walls were in "distressed" black walnut antique finishes in an overall French provincial décor. The columns of the Dining Room had already been sheathed in mirrors by 1941.

The original dark wood lattice-back chairs of the 1925 Dining Room had been painted ivory by the 1950s.

In 1974, a vestibule was added to the Ladies Dining Room as a buffer from kitchen distractions. In 1978, the name of room was changed to the Renaissance Room. In 1985, interior designer Logan Brown installed wallpaper that was the only reproduction of the original, located in the Brighton Pavilion in England.

In 1996, the design firm of Hosa Design Associates removed the false ceiling, and recreated the architecture (more or less) of the original 1925 design, but without its painted designs. Warm, honey-colored wood, Italian Verde marble wall base and a fireplace with a Romanesque mantle introduced new design elements into the room. Portraits of Reagan Distinguished American Award winners were hung in the recesses along the north wall that had once been windows to the outside.

On February 6, 2001, the room was renamed the Reagan Room in a ceremony held on the former president's 90th birthday. Former California Governor Pete Wilson represented Ronald and Nancy Reagan at the event.

The Reagan Distinguished American Award

The Jonathan Club presented a "Distinguished American" award to former President Ronald Reagan and Nancy Reagan in 1991, and the following year began a tradition of presenting The Reagan Distinguished American Award to recognize individuals for their contribution to the United States. Those receiving the award have, in the eyes of the Club, "demonstrated extraordinary qualities of leadership in their field of endeavor, and devotion of the values that have sustained our country since its founding."

In a formal ceremony with a military band in the Town Club's Main Dining Room each recipient is presented with a gold medallion created by Tiffany & Co. A portrait commissioned of each awardee is unveiled at the ceremony, and then permanently hung in the Reagan Room.

A portrait is commissioned of each recipient of the Reagan Distinguished American Award. The portraits are painted by Los Angeles representational artist and portraitist John Swihart, who was born in 1954. Swihart's work has been displayed in major exhibits all over the world. The Reagan Distinguished American Award recipients are: First row, President Ronald and Mrs. Nancy Reagan. Second row, (left to right) Bob Hope, Walter Cronkite and the Apollo 8 Astronauts: Frank Borman; James A. Lovell Jr.; William A. Anders. Third row: Coach John Wooden, Arnold Palmer and Elizabeth Hanford Dole. Fourth row: Secretary of State George Shultz, President Gerald R. and Mrs. Betty Ford, and Rev. Billy Graham.

THE FLORENTINE LOUNGE

This grand room was originally simply called the Lounge. In a 1925 Club brochure it was described as being of "Italian derivation, with old examples from Florentine palaces as the influence that inspired the wonderful arched door and mantel frames." By 1931, it was called the Main Lounge, and later the Florentine Lounge. Nothing has changed from its original 1925 state, except the furniture, draperies and wall coverings. Three identical massive carved wood forms surround the two doorways and the fireplace. Actually, the "wood" is cast plaster.

Fabric was added to the walls in 1981, by designer Logan Brown. The walls are upholstered with a damask woven in Belgium stretched over flannel. The installation of this upholstery was supervised by the same person Nancy Reagan used for her White House redecoration.

At one point in that mischievous period of design taste of the 1950s through the early 1970s the Club painted over the remarkable cobalt blue chandelier crystals. Perhaps this was done in 1973 when the chairman of the Planning and Improvement Committee wrote, "The existing lighting facilities will be restructured to a greater artistic advantage, with emphasis on enriching the details of the original chandeliers." The paint was cleared away and the crystals restored in the 1980s. The furnishings on the floor and the art on the walls have changed from one decade to the next as tastes have changed, but, aside from the upholstered fabric on the walls the shell of the room is little different than the room celebrated on opening day in 1925.

The room is used as a pre-function area for major events in the Main Dining Room and for special events such as weddings, bar and bat mitzvahs, corporate meetings and memorial services

In eight decades the basic character of the Lounge (later the Florentine Lounge) has remained the same. Only the changing furniture has hinted at the passage of time.

THE MAIN DINING ROOM
The Club's gathering site

In 1982, the artisians who retouched the original Smeraldi ceilings playfully added initials of friends in the Jonathan Club. At least seven sets of intitals can be found among the crests over the Main Dining Room. Here the initials BHJ are visible.

The Main Dining Room is one of the rooms least changed by the passage of eight decades. Today, except for the draperies, the room is essentially the same as the site where Club members gathered in 1925 to celebrate their new quarters. The Club's opening brochure describes a "heavy-beamed Italian ceiling and end walls of English paneling in oak," and "pierced crests of heavy bronze on...travertine side walls [performing] the dual purpose of ventilation and lighting fixtures."

During the boom days of the 1960s, daily breakfasts, lunches and dinners in the Main Dining Room required advance reservations. Today, the only regular meals are the Thursday night buffets. The room is popular for weddings and other special events.

The Club's largest and most formal events over the years have been staged in this venue. During the 1980s, buffets featured exotic meats, including rattlesnake, ostrich, zebra and lion. Each year, at a Junior Committee event, a boxing ring is erected among the glass chandeliers for a black-tie evening of boxing bouts that is almost always sold out. The Jonathan Breakfast Club meets here every Tuesday morning.

The room was air conditioned in 1941 and the ceiling was retouched in 1957 and 1968. In the 1980s, Giovanni Smeraldi's ceiling painting was restored. The board felt that the original colors were too bright and "folkloric" for the Italian Renaissance room so it directed that the original design be preserved but in a toned down palette. As the artisans restored the design they playfully hid at least seven sets of initials of favorite Club staff members in the crests.

In 1968, a movable dance floor was purchased. Prior to that time, a section of carpet was removed for dancing. In 1974, a vestibule was installed to buffer kitchen noises.

During the 1940s, when home refrigeration was not common, a game locker was maintained for members' storing of wild game, such as bear and deer. The Club would even dress and serve the meat for members upon request.

In 1954 the Board ruled that no member was to be allowed to furnish steaks for dinner, "wild game and fish excepted."

THE FOURTH FLOOR
A quiet setting for small meetings

The Fourth Floor has been an area of private dining rooms from the opening date of the building in 1925, but the layout of the floor has changed again and again over the years. Today, only three small private small rooms and a larger dining room occupy the floor as public rooms, instead of the seven private dining rooms of the original 1925 building. Back-of-the-house spaces have taken much of the space originally used for meeting rooms, and the garage addition of 1970 sealed off the north facing windows that once enhanced the rooms.

The Fourth Floor is a transitional floor, architecturally. It makes space for the upper part of the Third Floor Florentine Lounge and Main Dining Rooms, the lower part of the Fifth Floor swimming pool, the fifth level of the garage and food preparation space in addition to the private dining rooms.

The largest of the Fourth Floor Rooms was named the Marine Room, and it was here that the Tuesday morning Breakfast Club met for many years. In the mid-1950s, Jonathan Club member Arthur Beaumont was paid $2,250 to paint a mural along the east wall of the room. The mural depicts Juan Rodriguez Cabrillo's landing at San Diego Bay, becoming the first European to set foot in what is now California. Upon completion of the mural, in 1956, the room was renamed the Cabrillo Room.

In 1937, two of the smaller Fourth Floor rooms were named Orchid and Gold. In 1975, after interior design by Pat-Hugo Interiors, the names of the rooms were New England, New Orleans and West Indies. At that time, a space named the Plymouth Room became a fire escape corridor. In 1940, the lobby of the Fourth Floor was outfitted with a large radio. The floor was air conditioned in 1955.

In 1983, the rooms were again refurbished and renamed in honor of past presidents, Alexander, Huntington and Jeffries. In the smallest of these, the Jeffries Room, wallpaper entitled "The Monuments of Paris" was installed. Originally manufactured in 1814 in Paris by Joseph Dufour, the first set of this reproduction was placed on display at New York's Metropolitan Museum of Art. More than 1,000 silk screens were engraved to complete the printing before the screens were destroyed.

Upper photo: Lobby of the Fourth Floor

Lower photo: One of the many forms that meeting rooms took over the years.

Opposite: Cabrillo Landing by artist Arthur Beaumont

Arthur Beaumont
Cabrillo Landing, 1956
Oil on canvas glued to wall
Jonathan Club commissioned piece

Jonathan Club member Arthur Beaumont was paid $2,250 to paint this mural and was reimbursed the cost of costume rental and models. The scene depicts the landing at San Diego Bay of Juan Rodriguez Cabrillo, the first European to set foot in what is now California. This largest of the Fourth Floor meeting rooms was renamed the Cabrillo Room when Beaumont completed the mural in 1956.

The balcony over the gym disappeared with the dangling ropes from the ceiling. The orange basketballs painted in the keyholes led to the name "Pumpkin Garden" for the Fifth Floor gymnasium.

SPORTS AND FITNESS
The Club's midsection

The Jonathan Club made it clear upon opening its palatial quarters in 1925 that this was not an athletic club. Yet it devoted the entire Fifth Floor to sports and fitness and The Jonathan Club was reported to be "the first social club in the west to incorporate all the features of an athletic club into its home." All of the Town Club's competitive forums were built to non-regulation sizes, apparently to discourage the staging of tournaments that would attract non-members. The swimming pool was not half or quarter Olympic size, the basketball court was non-reg and the handball courts were off-sized (although they were modified to regulation size years later.)

The Fifth Floor contained far more lounges for sunning than pieces of aerobic equipment. The floor also contained a number of sleeping rooms, which were used as overflow rooms when other transient facilities were booked.

The early gym contained dangling ropes for climbing, medicine balls, wrestling mats and parallel bars. It also had "a mechanical horse of White House fame." There were no basketball backboards. And although there was less to watch in those early days there was a spectator's gallery in a balcony on the west side of the gym. One problem with the balcony was that volleyballs and basketballs were forever getting trapped there, delaying play until someone made the inconvenient trip to the Sixth Floor for their retrieval. The balcony was closed off, the seats removed, and the space was converted to a space for the 59er Club on the Sixth Floor…a group of 59 members formed in 1959.

Early aerobic equipment on the sun deck "for brief, snappy workouts" included rowing, cycling and saddle machines. Originally the roof area was topped with gravel, but was fitted with tile by the mid 1940s. Food was served both indoors and outdoors. Nude sunbathing was popular until taller buildings began to surround the club.

An important part of the athletic floor was the Turkish Bath Department, the portion containing wet and dry steam rooms, massage tables, foot vibrators, salt glows and other opportunities for inert activity. The Club prided itself on its therapeutic bath department where "the scientific…use of water…give[s] one the benefit of vigorous exercise without ever lifting a finger." In those days, the pool and Turkish Bath were open to members 24 hours a day. This practice ended in 1975. A Jacuzzi was added to the pool area in 1978.

In 1931, a backdrop was erected on the Fifth Floor roof so that golfers could practice their drives. The magazine article promoting this feature shows a member in a suit with dress shoes practicing his swing (talk about a dress code!)

A Violet-Ray room was installed in the mid-1930s, in which men proned themselves on tables, wearing dark goggles, while an attendant stood by under the same ultra-violet lights.

Originally a women's Turkish Bath section with lockers was provided on the Fifth Floor, but when the men needed more room the women were moved to the Sixth Floor, in the early 1940s. Women and family members were allowed to use the gym and pool on designated days. At other times men swam in the buff.

The Fifth and Sixth Floor sports and fitness areas underwent a major renovation in 1965-66. Walls, doors and ceilings were stripped down to structural steel and the floor was reconstructed, with acoustical ceilings, carpeting and updated lighting and fixtures. A salt-rub room and weight-lifting area were added indoors and a paddle tennis court and luncheon area added on the roof. Another extensive rehab of the space was completed in 1986-87, including a "fitness center," a wide expanse with occasional pieces of aerobic equipment "like pieces of sculpture" set against the walls.

In 1982, a running track was installed where cars had once parked on the roof of the parking structure. A few years later the track was banked, and paddle tennis courts were installed in the center of the track. In 1999, a "cardio theatre" of machines replaced what had been the aerobics floor, the wood floor was extended to create an area for weight lifting and weight machines and a rock climber were added.

A few decades ago, the gym had large orange basketballs painted on the keyholes, and to some people they looked like pumpkins. So, the Club figured that the Portland Trailblazers had their Rose Garden, the old Boston Garden was known originally as the Leprechaun Garden and Vermont had its Moss Garden. So the gym of the Jonathan Town Club became the Pumpkin Garden.

In 1981, the running track and paddle tennis courts displaced the roof parking on the roof of the 1970 parking structure addition.

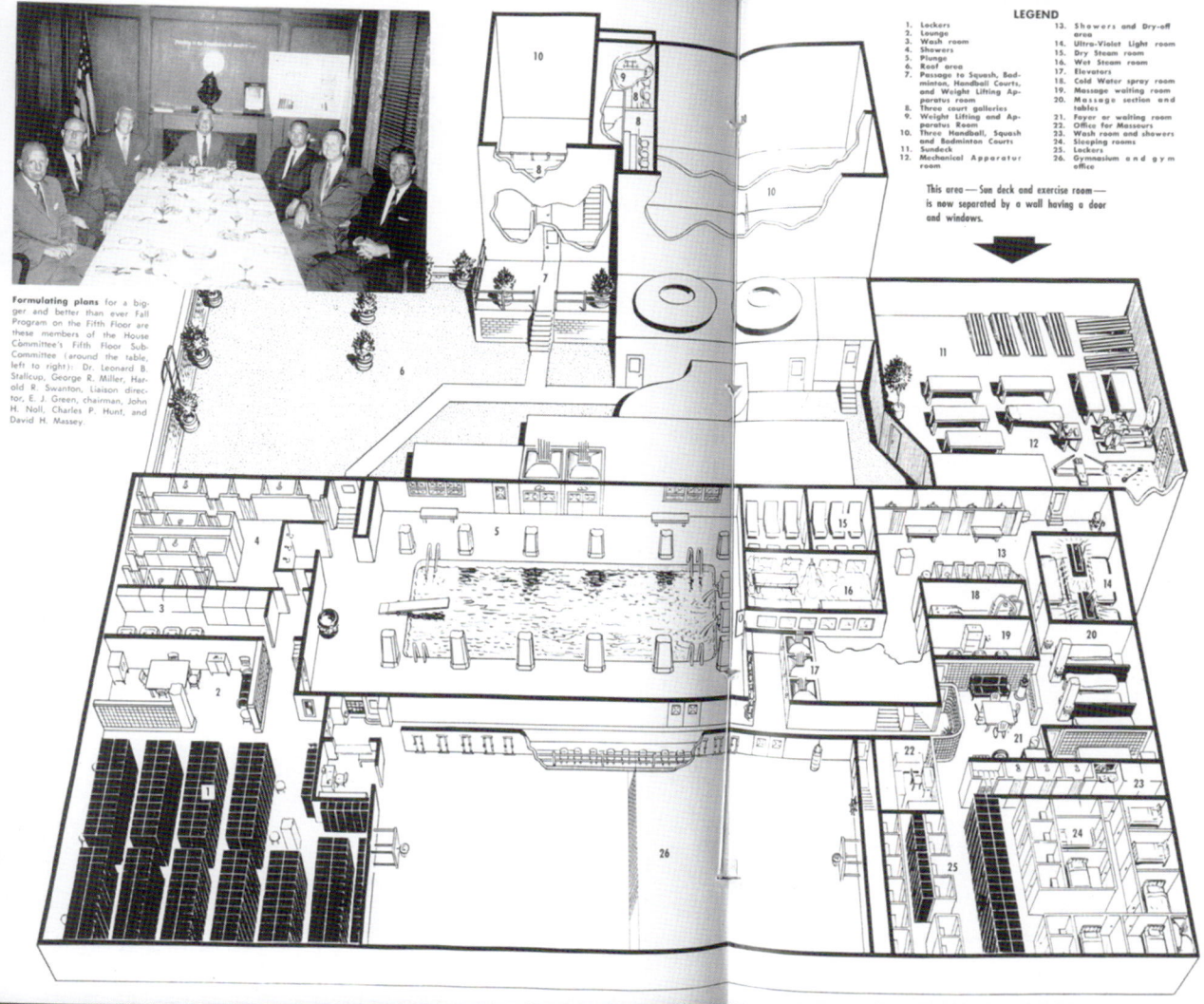

The fifth floor as it appeared in 1959

Today's Jonathan Club Suites are arguably the most luxurious overnight accomodations of any private club rooms in America.

RESIDENTIAL ROOMS

Important to the Town Club from the beginning

Today, one of the most distinguished elements of the Jonathan Town Club is its luxury overnight Suites. Overnight rooms have been an important part of the Jonathan Club since 1896, when the Club moved into three floors of 132 South Spring Street that had formerly been the Corfu Hotel. There were no overnight rooms in the original quarters at 130 South Spring Street, but there were residential rooms in the three clubhouses that followed. In 1915, a room in the Pacific Electric Building Club quarters rented for $30 a month (without private bath) or $82.50 a month for the most luxurious suite. By 1923, shortly before the Club moved to its current quarters, the rent had more than doubled.

The architect for the Town Club was Schultze and Weaver, the premier designer of hotels in the 1920s. The Jonathan Club was built on a hotel model, with a large lobby, front desk and six residential floors (Seven through Twelve) with a total of 250 overnight rooms…for use by men only.

The Seventh through Twelfth floors were mostly overnight rooms and twelve overnight rooms were built on the Sixth Floor. The Club's management offices were tucked away on the Sixth Floor, with the first floor street-adjacent space committed to retail rental. Some of the rooms were combined to form spaces that could serve uses beyond strictly overnight stays. One of these rooms, 1127, was abandoned during the Depression by its renters and in 1934 was converted to serve as the Club's board room, a use that has continued ever since. (The present board room table was specially designed for the room and installed in 1964.)

SIXTH FLOOR

During 1958 and 1959, after the Club's offices had been moved to the ground floor, the Sixth Floor was converted to club rooms for a variety of "social and business" groups. Among the spaces were gathering rooms for Junior Members, the Jonathan Yacht Club, the 614 Group (Shriners of the Al Malaikah Shrine), the Jovian Room (electrical group), the Army-Navy Group and the Communicators (publishing, advertising and public relations fields).

The balcony of the Fifth Floor gym, which had been reached through the Sixth Floor, was sealed off and converted to a space for the 59ers Club, a group of 59 (mostly younger) members formed in 1959.

Seventh Floor

In 1964, some of the Seventh Floor rooms were combined to form larger, well-decorated "executive suites" and conference rooms filling a need for various meetings. The single bedrooms on the Seventh Floor were redecorated in 1971 with a "woodsy, dark and very masculine feeling" according to their decorator, A. J. Stock of K. S. Wilshire, Inc. The Seventh Floor today contains a number of conference rooms and overnight rooms with the traditional club-type furnishings. The Yacht Club is also on the Seventh Floor.

In 1942, during the early part of World War II, blackouts were enforced to keep the city dark and invisible to enemy planes. The Club cleared out the Seventh Floor as a haven for families who were not able to return home at night.

Eighth and Ninth Floors

Sometime around 1960, the Eighth and Ninth Floors were abandoned, and left without carpeting. They were used as storage or left empty. Year after year, for four decades, boards of directors discussed plans to put the floors back into use, but the truth was that there was little demand for them as overnight rooms, meeting rooms or offices. In 1996, a collection of rooms on the Eighth Floor was used as a museum of the Club. In 2003, after four decades of abandonment, the Club borrowed $6 million and built out luxury Suites on the two floors.

Tenth Floor

The Tenth Floor today contains many rooms used for members who plan to be at the club for a few months or longer.

Eleventh Floor

The Eleventh Floor contains overnight rooms decorated with traditional club-type furnishings.

Gideon Bibles were placed in sleeping rooms, at no expense to the Club, in 1951.

The rooms have been updated again and again, and the concept of luxury suites has been introduced repeatedly. In 1941, the Club bragged of a stylish innovation for the rooms: Venetian blinds!

Residential rooms have shown the passage of time as graphically as have any rooms in the Town Club.

Opposite: A post-World War II update of the residential rooms.

KEY MEN – A LEGACY OF CLUB DWELLERS

A 2003 USC web site offering a Downtown Los Angeles Walking Tour chose to describe the venerable Jonathan Club as "home to a number of elderly gentlemen." This narrow description of the Club was badly outdated. There had been times when hundreds of the Club's rooms were rented to members, but by 2003 there were only about a dozen extended stay members staying in the Club for more than a few weeks at any given time, and they included women as well as men, young and old, and even an occasional family with children.

In the Town Club at Sixth and Figueroa those who lived in the Club were once called Key Men. In 1937 they formed the Jonathan Key Men organization and met on the first Sunday morning of each month. During World War II the Key Men purchased $200,000 in Victory Bonds. By 2003 the tradition of shared breakfasts was long past and the name Key Man was no longer in use. Those who stay at the Club for a few weeks or longer today generally fall into two categories: Those who have suffered a change in their relationship (separation, divorce or death of a mate) or those who have been forced out of their suburban home because of a natural disaster or "unnatural disaster" (known colloquially as "remodeling").

As the Town Club building was being constructed in 1924 a resident of the Pacific Electric Jonathan Club, Newton Potter, was so determined to have a room that suited him in the facility that he climbed eleven floors on ladders up the steel skeleton. He settled on Room 1131 because it would have a large closet. Otto Wuerker was one of the members to live in all three Jonathan facilities with residential rooms, 132 South Spring, the Pacific Electric Building and the Town Club at Sixth and Figueroa. Wuerker, a prominent jeweler at the turn of the nineteenth century, said he would have lived in the Club in its original Spring quarters if there had been overnight rooms. Major Chester Denham, who died in 1987, lived in the Club for 49 years.

Many of the Club's rooms were occupied permanently by members who either lived in the Club or who kept a downtown room. In the 1940s as many as 172 members resided at the Club at one time. Some residential rooms had their own showers; others did not. The last room rented to a member who had to traipse down the hall for a shower was in the late 1990s.

L. Ewing Scott had a residential room at the Jonathan Club on May 16, 1955, when his wife went missing. Her body was not found, but Scott was convicted of murder. He was convicted on evidence such as the discovery of her false teeth in Scott's back yard incinerator, and Scott spent the rest of his life in prison. After Jonathan Club employees came across a trunk with Scott's name on it three years after the disappearance, detectives got a search warrant and opened the trunk, wondering if it might contain the remains of Scott's missing wife. There were body parts in the trunk, but alas for the hopeful detectives, they were nothing more than strands of Scott's mother's hair that she had sent him some years earlier.

By the mid-1980s extended stay residents were housed on the Tenth and Eleventh Floors. In 1984 they were consolidated on the Tenth Floor, freeing the Eleventh Floor for transient rentals during the Olympic Games.

For most of the Club's history as a men's club women guests in the overnight rooms were strictly forbidden. This presented problems which the board wrestled with over the years. What to do about a female nurse caring for an ailing Club resident? Later, in the 1960s, when rooms on the Twelfth Floor were converted to office use, could female secretaries be on the upper floors of the building? The prohibition against adults of the opposite gender being in a Club residential room together was repealed in the mid-1970s.

Today extended stay guests are limited to a few rooms on the Tenth Floor. Many of these wouldn't even know the term "Key Man" or the tradition of large numbers of members living in the Club as in days of old.

Today's Cape Cod Room on the Thirteenth Floor is closed in and is still cursed with the dropped ceilings and modernized posts of post-World War II "improvements." In 1925 this was the roof, not the Thirteenth Floor, and was designed (so far as the public knew) as a Solarium, opening to the outside at the column line.

The Thirteenth Floor is now a closed-in floor like the rest, not the roof Solarium of the mid-1920s.

THIRTEENTH FLOOR
The floor that doesn't fit

The Town Club was promoted as a twelve-story building because the building was built to precisely 150 feet, the height limit of the day. The elevators and fire escapes went only to the Twelfth Floor. When the building was built in 1925 the roof was fitted out as a Solarium, "glazed in and comfortable." In later years, as the height limit was increased, the roof could be called the Thirteenth Floor and the service elevator could be brought up to that level.

For twenty years, from 1905 to 1925, The Jonathan Club had lived at the top of the city, in one of the highest floors in Downtown Los Angeles, in the Pacific Electric Building at Sixth and Main Streets. A commanding view of the city had become part of the identity of the Club, yet the dining rooms were placed low in the new Town Club building and the breathtaking view was designed for a very minor use. Not only was it a minor use, but it was off limits to all but card-carrying members.

The Town Club was built during the Depression. Was The Jonathan Club's Thirteenth Floor a speakeasy with liquor and gambling? Was the small bastion at the south end of the floor, now known as the Sky Bar, a room that could be easily sealed off at a moment's notice?

Although the plans for the roof show huge fans within this suspicious room, there are no ducts shown on the original blueprints passing through to the floor below, and it is clear in inspecting today's Sky Bar floor and the 12th Floor ceiling below it that no air shafts were ever constructed there.

The Jonathan Town Club was designed by architects Schultze and Weaver who are known to have created false walls and secret spaces in the nearby Biltmore Hotel which opened a year earlier. In a back corner of the Biltmore's Crystal Ballroom Schultze and Weaver designed a waist-high door that hid a secret stairway and catwalk that could quickly swallow people who'd been reveling with illegal alcohol. From that catwalk one could peek out of a peephole designed into the ornamental décor to see whether the police raiding party had left. The hotel's Presidential Suite was designed with secret panels for hiding bottles. If these architects designed such Prohibition dodges in a public hotel, they certainly could have planned for clever ruses in a private club!

One senior member of the Club today clearly remembers his father's stories about drinking there during Prohibition. All of the clues point to an exclusive area with no visitors where any raid by police would have had one floor's warning and time to seal off the evidence.

A sun deck on the east side of the floor was walled in in 1947 and the mysterious fan room was converted into a bar with its own fireplace. For years slot machines were installed in the room, and older members today remember seeing them in use by a Los Angeles mayor who was publicly fighting gambling at the time, and by the Los Angeles County sheriff. A television room was created in 1965.

The large room on the Thirteenth Floor has gone by many names. It was called Topside, the Roof Garden, the Top Deck and the Sky Room. In 1943, an elaborate seafood bar was installed there and the room took the name The Oyster Bar. In 1944, the name was changed to the Cape Cod Room.

Again and again in the years since Prohibition the Club has studied bringing elevators all the way up to the Thirteenth Floor. In 1940, the Club president announced that the decision had been made. In 1960, a lift again was proposed between the Twelfth and Thirteenth Floors. In 1964, the board considered installing an escalator between the Twelfth and Thirteenth Floors.

After "a complete Face Lifting and refurnishing" in 1941, telephone and lunch service was offered to those sunning themselves, often in the buff.

The apparent reason for limiting the Thirteenth Floor traffic to members died with Prohibition, yet the tradition continued. In 1967, the Board relaxed the rules and allowed guests after 3:00 p.m., but the protests of the members were so great that the liberalized rule was retracted a year later. Today, the members-only rule still applies at lunch time.

After laws were passed in the late 1990s prohibiting smoking in buildings, the Thirteenth Floor Sky Bar took on new importance as the gathering of the Club's Cigar Society.

Was there gambling in the Club? Bet on it!

There is only circumstantial evidence that there was organized, Club-sponsored drinking during Prohibition. But there is no question that there was gambling in the Club's past. There is repeated reference to slot machines in the Club's board minutes and older members can recall slot machines in the Club until the late 50s or early 60s.

In 1932 the board ordered all slot machines taken out of the Club "with the exception of the ones in Club rooms for which the Club is not responsible." The sports and fitness jocks protested, asking that the slot machines be left on the Fifth Floor to help create an athletic fund. (Perhaps the machines were viewed as a workout device for the right arm.) The board held firm.

The popular "Jazz on the Roof" summer evenings are staged on the Thirteenth Floor's Tuscan Terrace.

In 1935 a number of members asked for reimbursement for monies lost at a Club Hi-Jinks event. At a special meeting the board refused to consider the claims and, further, banned not only gambling games, but future Hi-Jinks events.

It is clear that the 1932 action of the board to rid the Club of slot machines did not have a lasting effect because on September 8, 1942, the vice detail of LAPD came calling on the Jonathan Club, because of "numerous complaints." Officers seized five slot machines, ranging from nickel to $1 devices, and arrested a bartender, Frank Erdman, 60. Acting as gentlemen in a gentlemen's club, the officers did not "molest" the "Club guests found playing the devices," according to the *Los Angeles Times*. At the trial, Judge Arthur Guerin fined the machines' asserted owner, bartender Fritz Godfrey, 50, a sum of $250 and 30 days in jail. He suspended the sentence on the condition that Godfrey sell the machines outside the State of California, with the proceeds going to the U.S.O. said the *Times*. Why was one bartender arrested and another put on trial? Why were machines in the Club owned privately by employees? The *Times* offers no hint.

Five years later the manager was "authorized to purchase two additional amusement machines for stand-by use."

Slot machines were still paying off in the Club through the 1950s, in the Thirteenth Floor Sky Bar and in the old Second Floor Men's Bar, despite a 1950 declaration to the Chief of Police to the contrary.

Evidently, the members weren't the only ones gambling in the Club. In 1941 the manager was instructed that employees using club telephones for horse racing calls were subject to dismissal.

Chapter 5
DEPRESSION

- 1929 – Stock Market crash, Oct. 29
- 1929 – UCLA moves to Westwood campus
- 1930 – Los Angeles population: 1,238,048
- 1930 – Jonathan Club purchases the old Edgewater Club in Santa Monica for use as a beach club
- 1930 – The Jonathonian magazine started. Name soon changed to The Jonathan.
- 1932 – Franklin Roosevelt elected President
- 1932 – Tenth Olympiad staged in Los Angeles
- 1933 – Prohibition ended
- 1933 – Long Beach earthquake does no serious damage to Town Club
- 1933 – Breakfast Club, first Club-within-the-club, formed

THE DEPRESSION BRINGS THE CLUB TO ITS KNEES

On November 24, 1930, Jonathan Club member W. Bunker Rossetti left his wife and one-year-old son, saying that he was on his way to his office. Instead, the 28-year-old stock broker went to the Club. Rossetti was in a happy marriage and was a serious athlete who had played football and lacrosse at Rutgers and had won many medals for swimming and diving. Once at the Club on this November morning he wrote five letters, sealed them and changed into his swimming trunks. He crawled out the window and made his way to the sixth floor ledge where he took his competitive diving stance. He executed a swan dive onto Figueroa Street narrowly missing two cars and died instantly on impact. The Depression was in full swing.

In the days and weeks following the stock market crash of October 29, 1929, The Jonathan Club had underestimated the dire impact of that event, just as the majority of the American public had. Times had been so good in the Roaring Twenties that most people were sure that the financial skies would clear after this pesky little economic squall had cleared away. How wrong American society was. And how wrong those leading the Jonathan Club were! The Depression would worsen and worsen, and one member after another sooner or later concluded that the luxury of a membership in an exclusive private club was too much for the budget of a family in financial ruin.

After the stock market crash of October 29, 1929, no hint of hard times shows up in the board minutes until May of 1930, when the board took its first bold step towards generating cash. It raised the dues of widows.

Perhaps that's not a fair statement. The board had presented to the membership, and the membership had approved at its annual meeting two weeks earlier, a new structure for membership designed to bring in cash. But the tiny dues increase for widows is the first recorded action of the board acting alone to bring in more cash after the stock market crash.

At the May 12, 1930, annual meeting, the Club created a $2,500 Regular Life Membership classification allowing a member to live dues-free for the rest of his life. Another category of $1,000 Special Life Member, with monthly dues, was also created. Both of the Life Membership categories allowed the right to transfer the membership and both provided for preferential pay-off in case the Club was dissolved. Resident Membership was pegged at $500. Junior Membership for sons aged ten through 21 would be $10.

Within three months of the stock market crash an increasing number of members were leaving the Club. Among the earliest to leave was Leonard Schultze, the Town Club architect. His partner, Fullerton Weaver, soon quit the Club too. The era of grand skyscrapers and luxury hotels was unmistakably over, and with it the demand for architects to design such buildings.

William Jeffries knew only one way to think: Big. Following on the heels of the glory he had won by erecting the Town Club at Sixth and Figueroa he dreamed another dream: A presence on the Santa Monica Beach. In 1930, with a Depression darkening the world all around, he boldly purchased an institution that had gone bankrupt in the very best of times. At a time when The Jonathan Club was hunkering down to survive the 99-year lease and payments on two bond issues on the Town Club, Jeffries saddled the Club with another 99-year lease and yet more debt.

Jeffries and his board formed the Jonathan Beach Club, Ltd., paying $442,220.85 for the Santa Monica property and taking on an obligation of $1,500 a month on the 99-year lease. All of the capital stock in Jonathan Beach Club, Ltd., was owned by The Jonathan Club. Not only did he purchase the Edgewater Club, but ambitiously bought two large pieces of real estate immediately north of the Edgewater as well, the 'Zuckerman' parcel for $100,000 and the 'Gertrude L. Seaver' lot for $60,000. William P. Jeffries, with Club Secretary J. C. Rendler, Board Member J. W. Jump, R. D. Robinson and E. R. Carpenter, borrowed $430,000 for the real estate deals. The Edgewater purchase was approved by the board on May 6, 1930.

- 1933 — Ladies Dining Room (now Reagan Room) name changed to Parisienne Room, celebrating end of Prohibition
- 1934 — Name of Parisienne Room (now Reagan Room) changed to Blue Room
- 1934 — Original Jonathan Beach Club proves too expensive. Arrangements for members made at Grand Hotel instead
- 1935 — April 10, "The Jonathan Club" sold on court house steps. "Jonathan Club" replaces it. Club buys land under Town Club which was formerly leased. First beach club (Edgewater Club) lost
- 1935 — Sea Breeze Club/Beverly Beach Club purchased as new beach club

Throughout the Depression the Club kept up its celebrated high life. Though fewer and fewer were able to afford the Club and its activities, those who could looked forward to the same elegant events that had always distinguished The Jonathan Club.

Clearly, the Club was not reading the economic tea leaves correctly. When a special board meeting had been called for April 24, 1930, to purchase of the Edgewater Club only one director had voted no. At the annual meeting on May 12, Jeffries had discussed at length the purchase of the Edgewater Club and surrounding property and the members assembled "heartily approved" the purchases, according to the minutes. Nine days later Jeffries was re-elected president, there having been no other nominations.

Jeffries had acted independently, as a leader who had far outdistanced his followers. There is no record of Club elections for directors between 1925 and 1930, or any record of the board bothering to formally re-elect its officers during that period. Jeffries and his board ruled the Club with little check and no balance, and this oligarchy might have continued for some time longer had not a bothersome little Depression gotten in the way.

The Club struggled mightily to fill the 144 guest rooms of a seasonal beach resort while trying to keep its downtown rooms filled. The Club beat the drums to encourage members to take a week off with the family to vacation in Santa Monica.

On June 11, the board had approved bonded indebtedness of Jonathan Beach Club Company, Ltd. On July 16, the board had met for the sole purpose of borrowing even more money. When that still wasn't enough, Jeffries and his board saw no problem with their $275 assessment. After all, whatever the board had deigned in the past, the membership had obediently ratified. The Club had borrowed all it could from outside sources, so on July 29, 1930, the board decided to ask the membership to approve a $275 assessment. The sum of $250 would go to the Club, with the other $25 going to the Internal Revenue Service. A Special Meeting of the Membership was called for August 11, 1930, for a vote.

That August 11 meeting was momentous. No minutes exist in the Club archives, but subsequent minutes and reports paint a picture of a membership rebellion against Bill Jeffries and his board. From the floor the members appointed a Special Committee to look into the purchase of the beach properties and the overall financial condition of The Jonathan Club. The committee was composed of seven men: David W. Pontius, chairman, plus Rex Clark, E. J. Fleming, Speed S. Fry, W. H. Anderson, Dave F. Smith and Addison B. Day. A Members Committee was also appointed at this meeting, with the charge of recommending who should remain on the board and who should be asked to resign. The meeting was adjourned until August 21.

At the August 21 adjourned meeting, the Special Committee, also known as the Committee of Seven, reported back to the membership on the financial implications of the beach transactions. It offered a plan for digging the Club out of its crisis. Some members at the August 11 meeting had suggested turning back the Santa Monica property "to those from whom it was purchased." The Special Committee concluded sternly, "This positively cannot be done," noting that, for better or worse, "We now own a Club at the beach. It is the finest beach club on the Pacific Coast. It is as near Los Angeles as any other beach club. It can be operated at a reasonable cost." The report concluded that "The Beach Club property unquestionably will increase in value within the next several years." It was the Committee's opinion that the purchase would have had the approval of the majority of members had it "been worked out in the beginning in a more satisfactory basis." The Special Committee reported that if 90 percent of the Club's members agreed to this plan, Jeffries and his board would agree to personally take over the Zuckerman property.

In March, 1930, a car on the Southern Pacific Lark Limited was named "Jonathan Club" by the Pullman Company. This was one of two cars built especially for the elite train. The other was named "Family Club" in honor of a pretigious club in San Francisco. The Jonathan Club car was christened with a bottle of California wine over its coupling.

The Committee said that while the $275 assessment that the board had tried to railroad through was "the wrong way to approach the matter," the committee nevertheless concluded that it was necessary, and it suggested a way of giving the members, and the Club, something more in return. It proposed that the assessment carry with it a transferable membership certificate which could be sold to another person for $50. Or the certificate could be used for a junior membership for a member under 30 years of age. Or the $275 could be applied on a $500 non-transferable membership, to a prospect approved by the board. Thus, the Club would receive an infusion of cash from the assessment, and a windfall of new members paying monthly dues, providing even more cash. The members approved the assessment plan. The "complimentary" members still had to run the gauntlet of the membership process and about ten percent of those suggested were turned down by the Membership Committee.

At this same August 21 meeting, Rex B. Clark presented the Members Committee report recommending that William Jeffries and George Belsey resign. Interestingly, there is no formal record of Belsey being elected to the board in the first place, so casual were the assumptions of leadership by the Jeffries board. There are no minutes of the August 21 meeting either. What we know of its actions comes from later board minutes. At the board meeting of September 3, Jeffries was not present, and Director Gordon Jump presided. The board systematically listed the actions taken by Jeffries in connection with the beach property purchases and assumed full responsibility for the Club action by action.

At the next regular meeting, on September 10, William Jeffries and George Belsey submitted their resignations. The Jeffries era had come to an ignoble end. The man who had catapulted the Club into such prestige and prominence with its magnificent 12-story downtown monument had rolled the dice in a double-or-nothing play for a second grand shrine on the Santa Monica sand. And lost. It would take the Club a decade to dig out of the hole that Jeffries had put it in, and it couldn't start climbing out while Jeffries was still digging. Ever so reluctantly the Club had to displace a leader it had held, and still held, in affection. The Club named Jeffries President Emeritus to show that there were no hard feelings, and Jeffries remained active in The Jonathan Club until he died. On the same day the Club replaced William Jeffries with Dave Smith at the helm the board decided to pay debts under $510, put money into escrow for the general contractor for the Town Club, and "instead of 25 cents on the dollar, Club officers to negotiate with each individual creditor" for larger amounts owed by the Club. The Depression had hit the Club in a way it could no longer deny.

On September 11, a momentous special meeting of the membership was held. Director Dave Smith presided in this first day of the new era. The $275 assessment was approved, membership caps were optimistically waived, and the members began to prepare for the worst. In case of liquidation, Regular Life Members would get $2,000 and Special Life Members would get $500. The remainder of the funds would be divided equally among Regular Life, Special Life and Resident members. Members at this meeting flooded the proceedings with other bylaw amendments. Some passed; some did not. Two amendments were proposed to curb the power of the board and give the membership broader say but both were defeated.

At the end of the meeting the members gave the Member Committee a standing ovation for its work in changing the leadership of the Club. The Club responded to the Depression in a number of ways. The board:
- re-started *The Jonathan*, to communicate better and bolster enthusiasm for the Club.
- lowered prices.
- eliminated the membership cap to make room for the complimentary memberships.
- saved $659.60 by not updating members' numbers.
- cut credit for all members back to $500.
- quit mailing chits to members and held the chits for a month for members' inspection.
- installed pay phones on each floor to stem the expense of members' use of Club phones.
- reduced the rent significantly for the Town Club's retail spaces along Figueroa.

By October 29, 1930, exactly one year after the Stock Market crash, 75 percent of The Jonathan Club members had paid their $275 assessments. By August 31, 1931, 92 percent had paid their assessments. On October 7, 1931, the board suspended 127 members who had still not paid their assessments and later that month began court proceedings against 100 members who owed the Club money. By December 31, 96 accounts had been assigned for collection. In 1932, the board granted leniency for members with 25 years tenure if "through adverse circumstances" they were unable to pay their dues.

As the Town Club's first mortgage bonds were about to go into default a bond holders' protective committee was formed and began negotiating a refinancing plan. The committee was willing to consider a refinancing plan if the Club agreed to offer the Town Club's furniture as collateral. The Club's board agreed.

The Club was desperate for cash and for members. It got cash from members in two opposite ways. It offered life memberships for immediate cash, with the promise of no monthly dues, and it offered memberships at low initiation fees to get the monthly dues. Initiation fees were lowered to $50, then to $25. In some of the Depression-era policies the initiation fee dropped to zero, at one point requiring a check for six months dues in advance. At one point the secretary of the Club, J. C. Rendler, resigned from the board to assume a paid position of commissioned salesman for membership development.

On a single day, March 31, 1933, 116 members were suspended for non-payment, including a member of one of Southern California's most prominent families, Carl Phineas Banning. As it turned out, this bleak day was but a harbinger of the six months to come.

June 28, 1933 – 133 resignations were accepted
July 12, 1933 – 63 resignations were accepted
July 26, 1933 – 34 resignations were accepted
August 11, 1933 – 81 resignations were accepted
September 6, 1933 – 44 resignationswere accepted
September 22, 1933 – the board accepted 51 resignations and suspended 178 other members for a total of 229 crossed off the roster in a single board meeting.

During the early years of the Depression, the membership rolls had soared because of the provision that with the $275 assessment came one free membership. However, these new members had not been men naturally attracted to the Club, but prospects who had cashed in on a good deal or had come in on a lark. In many cases there was no long-term interest or cultural fit in the Club, and the complimentary members began dropping out in droves as their interest in the Club waned or their ability to pay the monthly dues fizzled out.

The overall membership net gain or loss for the first five years of the Depression were: 1929 -14; 1930 +228 (increased because of the free memberships); 1931 +1,115; 1932 -747; 1933 -1,225; 1934 -1,052; 1935 -195. The net loss from the time of the crash through 1935 was a staggering 1,890 members with a drop of 2,277 in the two-year period 1933-34.

The kingdom of The Jonathan Club was tumbling down everywhere. The Club could not make its payments on the debt of the Town Club and was losing its Beach Facility and surrounding properties in Santa Monica. It could not repay its bank loans on schedule and its membership was plummeting. It was running out of money and running out of members. The end was near.

THE END AND THE BEGINNING

Sold on the courthouse steps

The board which the membership had installed because of William Jeffries' high handed governance now took its own autocratic liberties. On May 8, 1933, the board chose its own directors without going to the membership for an election. The board then chose a new president to save the Club from its freefall to ruin. Its choice was LeRoy M. Edwards, a corporate law attorney who had come onto the board in 1930 as part of the housecleaning team. The former president, Dave F. Smith, a veteran of the old Jeffries board who had then led the Club since Jeffries' ouster, stepped down to the role of treasurer. Could Edwards save the Club? The turnaround came under Edwards' leadership but perhaps not in the way he envisioned. A month after taking office, he retained the law firm of Gibson, Dunn & Crutcher to craft the legal framework for a financing plan, but if this was the plan that was finally used it took almost two years to implement.

After Edwards became president the Club struggled to make the payments on both its first and second trust deeds. The Club tried to convince 65 percent of the second trust deed holders to accept a plan to refinance their bonds and offer a lower payment scheme, apparently without success. Edwards struggled for a year and a half to put a refinancing plan in place. In November of 1934, the board minutes mention communications with Pacific Mutual Life Insurance Company, and from that point on an elaborate plan by that firm began to unfold.

The Jonathan Club Building Company, Ltd., held the leasehold interest on the land under the Town Club, the fee interest on nearby lots, and the furniture and fixtures of the Town Club. On February 1, 1935, Jonathan Club Building Company, Ltd., defaulted a semi-annual payment of $33,052.50 on bonds totaling $1,017,000. The default triggered a foreclosure action by the Pacific Mutual Life Insurance Company. Years later, a Jonathan Club Law Committee explained that, while the insurance company had caused the foreclosure, "it acted independently, merely as [a] creditor...without seeking or having the cooperation or consent of The Jonathan Club..."

On March 30, 1935, Club president LeRoy Edwards wrote members of the Club advising them that events were about to unfold which would leave the club in possession of the land under the Town Club, land which was currently being leased. The upcoming events would leave "the corporate structure radically simplified" leaving "but one owning and operating corporation" instead of three (The Jonathan Club, Jonathan Club Building Company, Ltd. and Jonathan Club Beach Company). Edwards promised, "[t]here will be no interruption in the use of the facilities of the Club by its members." He wrote "We are advising you at this time of the plan being effected, so that there will be no confusion in your mind as to the ultimate results of any proceedings which you may hear of being taken, and so that you need have no fear of any assessment being levied upon you." The "proceedings" he spoke of so mysteriously unfolded 10 days later.

The foreclosure initiated by Pacific Mutual caused the sale of The Jonathan Club outside the eastern entrance of the Hall of Justice at Temple and Spring Streets at 11:00 a.m. on April 10, 1935, where The Jonathan Club was put on the block to the highest bidder. And who should show up at the east entrance of the Hall of Justice but officials of the Pacific Mutual Life Insurance Company, who offered the high bid of $308,935.60.

On April 16, 1935, Pacific Mutual sold its acquisition to "Jonathan Club," the organization it had set up for this purpose, for $1,135,000. The new Jonathan Club then purchased from the old club its inventories of food and beverages, its accounts receivable, the now worthless stock of Jonathan Building Company and the Jonathan Beach Club obligations for certain bank loans.

The foreclosure had extinguished the security of First Mortgage Bonds of Jonathan Club Building Company. Holders of these First Mortgage Bonds were offered thirty cents on the dollar. The big losers in April of 1935 were the Second Mortgage Bond holders, who, in effect, lost their equity, relieving the reorganized club of an obligation of over a million dollars. The guarantor of these Second Mortgage bonds was the old club, by then defunct, not the new club.

Years later, in 1941, a suit was filed on behalf of First and Second Mortgage bond holders claiming that the Beach Club, old city club and the new city club were operated as one entity, and that the present club needed to make good on the old bonds. The suit claimed that the old and new clubs "had the same interests, purposes, business, were owned by the same persons, had identical officers, used the same official publication, were represented by the same attorneys, occupied the same offices, allowed their respective books to be under control of the same persons, used the same staff, used all of the properties jointly, used identical names, trade marks and letterheads, used the same account and utility companies and the same post office permits." "Nonsense!" Jonathan Club protested and in December, 1942, prevailed in court, firmly defending the principle that a new club had been established on April 10, 1935.

On May 1, 1935, the Club's Managing Committee considered two options for its Santa Monica presence. It could spend about $130,000 and acquire the title to the vacant properties around the old Edgewater Beach Club, or it could buy another club up the coast, the Beverly Beach Club, which was "fully equipped and ready to operate." The panel decided to buy the Beverly Beach Club, paying $125,000 for the facility that serves as the Jonathan Beach Club today.

The Jonathan Club Beach Company had defaulted on its rent in March 1934 and made no further payments. Now, in May, after the decision to buy the club up the beach, Jonathan Club removed its watchman, abandoning the property to the mortgage holder, Pacific Mutual Life Insurance Company. The Jonathan Beach Club (the old Edgewater Club) beach property was thus completely lost by foreclosure and trustee sale.

The Jonathan Beach Club Company, unable to make its mortgage payments, had conveyed its rights on the two other beach parcels in lieu of foreclosure proceedings. The "Seaver" and "Zuckerman" properties had been lost before the transfer of Club assets in April, 1935.

On June 21, 1935, the new Jonathan Club purchased the former Beverly Beach Club (the former Sea Breeze Beach Club). Pacific Mutual Life Insurance Company lent the Club $125,000 for this purchase.

All of the members in good standing of the old Jonathan Club were offered membership into this new Jonathan Club, and the old membership certificates were cancelled. The new club, with its Pacific Mutual board, hired the board of the old Jonathan Club to act as its Operating Committee.

The reorganization, as momentous as it was in terms of legal proceedings, was virtually invisible to the Club's membership. *The Jonathan* magazine carried no mention whatsoever of the cosmic forces destroying and resurrecting its Town Club. The magazine continued to list the same board of directors and even continued to describe the publishing entity as The Jonathan Club (not Jonathan Club, the organization's new name).

Although their photographs are on no wall in the Club, and their names are on no lists of former directors and officers, they were, technically, the original directors and officers of the Club that exists today:

President: John B. Cooley

Vice President: Nolan S. Coogan

Secretary: T. S. Burnett

Ass't Secretaries: Ryno Dahlstrom, W. S. Watts

Treasurer: T. S. Burnett

Ass't Treasurers: Elmer C. Potter, Lester Pando

Separate minutes were kept for the new club and for the board which had served the old club. The Pacific Mutual board and officers who had served the transitional Jonathan Club resigned on August 7, 1935, as a tree falling in a forest. Their role had been invisible to the membership of the Club. The old Jonathan Club board, which was the only board visible to the membership throughout the transition, was now officially back in charge. The rank and file member probably didn't know that any other leadership team had been in titular command.

The Depression was not over. Hard times were ahead and the Club had trouble meeting its new obligations, even though this burden was ever so much lighter than that of the early 1930s. But by negotiating with creditors the Club made it through the rest of the decade. Membership slowly climbed in every year for the rest of the decade, little by little the economy improved and little by little the Club's financial health got better.

The Club had weathered what would prove to be its Hundred Year Storm.

Chapter 6
JONATHAN CLUB AT THE BEACH

LIFE ON THE BEACH

Life on the Santa Monica beach started for The Jonathan Club on April 21, 1927, when two proposals were submitted to the board. One proposal was for a Club site in the Holcomb Valley for fishing, swimming and boating. The other was from a bankruptcy trustee submitting information on the failed Edgewater Club of Southern California. Almost exactly three years later, in a worsening Depression, President William Jeffries, without checking with the membership, obligated the Club to what he felt was a bargain and an opportunity. The board formed the Jonathan Beach Club Company, Ltd., as the entity which would control the beach interest in the same way that the Jonathan Club Building Company controlled the Town Club. William Jeffries bought the Edgewater Club and the vacant land around it.

The Edgewater Club, built at the same time as the Town Club, in much the same style, was an elegant facility, a perfect companion for the large formal presence of The Jonathan Club in Downtown Los Angeles. In another economic climate, and with better communications with the membership, it might have been a good match. But there was a depression raging outside. The new debt threatened to put the Club under, and it ultimately did. Jeffries lost his office because of the purchase.

The Jonathan Club's first Santa Monica facility was located at the foot of Pico Street where the Shutters Hotel stands today. The building that once served as the Jonathan Beach Club was razed in 1964.

In retrospect one wonders how Jeffries thought this could ever work. He had bought a monstrous seven-story club building with 144 overnight rooms to fill. The club he bought had had the advantage of a membership completely oriented to the beach, yet the club had failed in the very best of times, in the boom of the Roaring Twenties, well before the Stock Market crash. The Jonathan Club did its best to promote the beach club and fill its rooms, but it was a struggle from the beginning, and to make matters worse Santa Monica suffered two unusually cold summers. In 1933, desperate to unload its white elephant, the Club employed a consultant to find another club or hotel operator to take over the property. The consultant wrote back saying "I have...failed to find even a slight interest."

After four catastrophic years, the Club abandoned its huge building and sold its furniture, but by now, Jonathan Club members had come to expect a Santa Monica Beach benefit, so the Club arranged privileges at the Grand Hotel.

The Jonathan Club was sold on the courthouse steps on April 10, 1935, and two months later the reorganized club bought the facility that had been opened in 1926 as the Sea Breeze Beach Club and operated briefly as the Beverly Beach Club. *The Jonathan* magazine described the new beach home of the Jonathan Club with excitement, including its "beautiful swimming pool" of "sheltered calm water," "bather's grill," "main dining room," "attractive esplanade running the full length of the clubhouse," "cocktail room" with its "knotty pine paneling" and "spacious locker rooms and showers."

Almost immediately the shoreline changed at both the old and new Jonathan Beach Clubs. A breakwater was constructed in 1933 which washed away the beaches to the south, where the old Edgewater Beach Club was, and deposited the beaches to the north, where the new Jonathan Beach Club was. The clubs to the south were angered to lose their beaches and the clubs to the north were upset that the ocean was now so far away from their steps. When the Jonathan Club first moved into the old Sea Breeze Beach Club, the ocean was only 75 feet away from the clubhouse.

In 1931, the Club magazine reported, "There have been complaints made by members regarding bathers doing away with the 'uppers' of their bathing suits. The complaints have been made especially against adults. While there is a city ordinance against leaving off the 'uppers,' the Board of Directors has not tried to enforce the regulation, but have left the matter entirely to the discretion of the members." The article was referring to the tops of men's swim suits.

Again and again, the board tried to unload the beach club, feeling it was not important enough to the Town Club to justify its expense. The first of these efforts came in 1943, when President Louis Canepa sold the Jonathan Beach Club for $125,000 subject to the ratification of the membership. The membership, however, voted *unanimously* to keep the Club and the purchase was nullified. Instead of unloading the beach club, the membership unloaded the president and board which had done the deal.

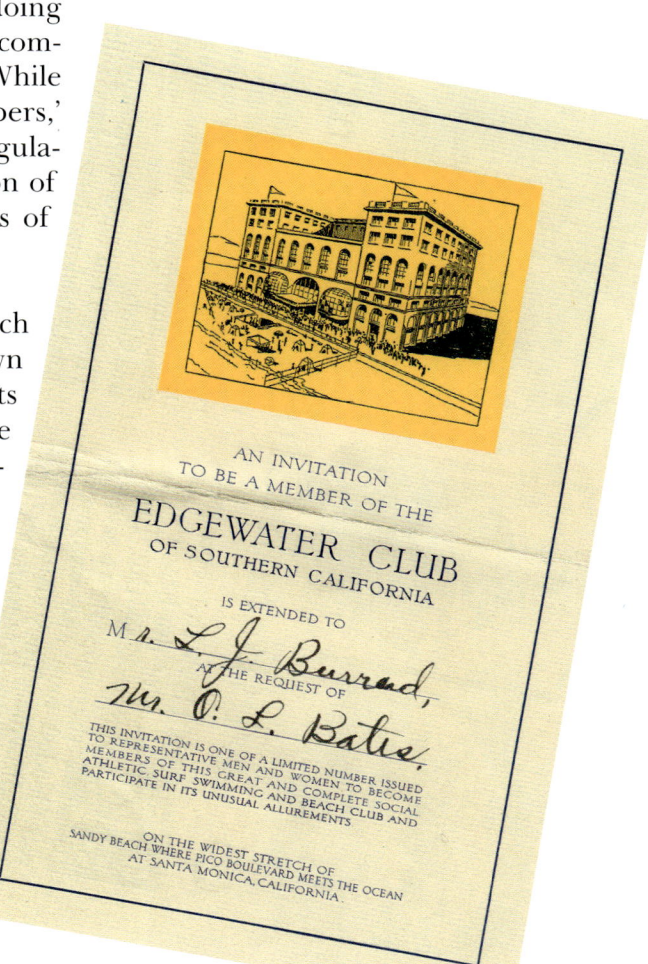

EDGEWATER CLUB

Ground was broken for the Edgewater Club of Southern California on January 4, 1925, and the club opened as portions were completed in the spring of 1926. It rose from the Santa Monica beachfront, nested between two similar-sized clubs, the Del Mar Club to the south and the Breakers to the north. The Edgewater Club was located at the foot of Pico, where the Shutters Hotel stands today.

Billing itself as "the foremost Beach Club in the World," it was built as a year-round "social, beach and athletic club" in a period when grand clubs were springing up all along the Santa Monica coastline. Even in the booming, roaring 1920s there were not nearly enough private club prospects for all of these competitors.

In pondering the magnificent details of the Edgewater Club building, keep in mind that these also describe the first Jonathan Beach Club of 1930.

The Edgewater Club offered 212 feet of fenced-off beach for its private use with a tunnel under the public boardwalk so that members would not suffer the discomfort of mixing with the general public on their way from private club to private beach. A club lifeguard watched this private surf from a blue and gold tower. On the beach side of the tunnel an esplanade for dining and lounging stretched the entire width of the property. The club bragged that "(t)he Esplanade of the Edgewater Club stands paramount – it is unequalled in any other club in the world and will undoubtedly be used as the standard for clubs of similar nature in the future." A Bather's Grill served the Edgewater's guests on the beach.

The club boasted a huge indoor plunge with heated seawater, said to be the largest indoor salt-water club pool in the United States, with three diving boards and a large diving platform. The Edgewater pool, open from 7 a.m. until midnight every day, was exactly twice the size of the Jonathan Town Club's pool, and the galleries beside the Edgewater pool could accommodate 500 spectators. The club even offered an Olympic champion, Ben Thrash, as a swimming coach for its members.

Courts for "Volley-ball" were "screened to guard those who are on the beach." Inside the club building were "the finest equipped gymnasium," boxing rooms, fencing rooms and massage rooms. Playrooms were provided for children. Handball and tennis courts were available on the roof.

Built in a Moorish style, it featured a large and ornate lobby, fitted with travertine walls and a hand-painted ceiling. The fifth and sixth floors housed the main social activities. The club featured a general Sun Lounge and other lounges for men and for women, private dining rooms, game rooms, billiard parlors and a library. The Mural Dining Room, on the Ocean Promenade, was open to both members and the general public, and was intended as a revenue generator for the club. Also planned were a beauty parlor, barber shop and storefront retail spaces ideal for "Drug Store and Sporting Goods" use.

The Main Dining Room could host 500 diners for breakfast, lunch and early dinner under its 21-foot ceiling, and an even more elegant room, the Marigold Supper Room, was open for late suppers. A highly polished dancing floor occupied half the room. The Marigold dining event was so magnificent that its orchestra was featured from 11:00 p.m. till midnight on a nightly radio show in which guests were introduced.

The sixth floor Auditorium came with a stage and a balcony and plans for "one of the finest organs in the United States." This giant room, ten times the size of the largest public room in the Jonathan Town Club, could accommodate an audience of 3,000 people, or 1,000 dancers. It was designed for use as a convention hall, dancing site, boxing arena, lecture hall or musicale theater.

Five floors were designed for sleeping quarters, "to accommodate 400 members." One floor housed suites and rooms for families, two floors were dedicated to male guests and one floor was set aside for women's sleeping rooms. The club contained 144 guest rooms and 100 dormitory rooms in six-person cubicles.

Life memberships were at first offered for $300, the price later rising to $500, $750 and finally $1,000. Dues-paying members paid $275 at the time the club was opened. Women were welcomed as members. Among the Edgewater's life members were Ed B. Tufts, a founding board member of The Jonathan Club, and LeRoy M. Edwards, the man who, as the Jonathan Club's president in the depth of the Depression, would engineer the sale of the old Edgewater facility after The Jonathan Club had acquired it. Others on the membership list included William Randolph Hearst, Rudolph Valentino, Walter W. Ralphs (Ralphs Grocery) and Carroll L. Post (Postum Cereal Co.).

"The Edgewater Club typifies stability," its promotional brochure had bragged in an ironic statement. In 1928, only two years after opening, and still in the flush economic boom of the Roaring Twenties, the club went bankrupt. According to the Los Angeles Times, the cause was "lack of unity of club members and mismanagement."

The life cycle of the Edgewater Club:

Edgewater Club – *Opened 1926. Bankrupt 1928.*
Cascades – *Opened 1928. Closed 1929.*
Jonathan Beach Club – *Opened 1930. Closed 1934.*
Army Air Forces Redistribution Station No. 3 – *Opened 1943 as a recovery center for Army Air Forces pilots on 20-day furloughs.*
Santa Monica Ambassador Hotel
Kabat-Kaiser Institute – *Opened 1948. A million dollar rehabilitation hospital for neuromuscular afflictions like polio, multiple sclerosis and arthritis, founded by Henry J. Kaiser, Jr., himself a victim of multiple sclerosis. Kaiser was the son of industrialist Henry J. Kaiser. Dr. Herman Kabat's technique had helped the younger Kaiser recover from his supposedly incurable condition. After the site fell into disuse it sat boarded and barricaded, its windows broken out. A drunk vagrant once fell down an elevator shaft. The former Edgewater Club, along with two other "white elephants" of the golden club era of the 1920s, was razed beginning in November of 1964.*
Shutters Hotel – *Opened 1993.*

Three of the major old Santa Monica North Beach clubs are visible in this postcard: The Breakers, The Edgewater Club and the Casa Del Mar. The Edgewater Club was later The Jonathan Beach Club.

In 1955, the board decided that in case of the sale of any Club property that a notice of the sale be published in *The Jonathan* magazine for a period of thirty days prior to the date of sale "for the purpose of permitting all members interested to submit bids." In 1956, the board considered selling the Beach Facility to a group of Club members "who would purchase this property as a private investment and make it available to the Club on a long-term lease." In 1960 and 1961, the board again seriously considered selling the beach facility. The Club surveyed the members and found that 72% of those returned favored keeping the Beach Club. As recently as 1988, the board voted on selling the Beach Club, and decided to keep it…by a vote of five to four.

All of this sounds inconceivable in light of the current success and popularity of the Beach Facility. In the ten years following the Northridge Earthquake of 1994, the Club invested over $11 million in the Beach Facility, which was more than it invested in the Town Club during the same period. The Beach Facility is a treasure, and is today is the primary reason why many people join the Jonathan Club.

Parking was always a problem as the Club negotiated with one adjacent owner after another for extra space for cars. In 1955, the Club purchased lots 130 and 131 adjacent to the Beach Club for $15,125.

In 1943, because of World War II, the Beach Facility was open only from 10:00 a.m. till 6:00 p.m., the swimming pool was drained and there was no food or beverage service. Members were encouraged to bring their picnic baskets and use the tables of the dining room. The pool was again filled for the 1944 season.

In 1944, a Bather's Cocktail Lounge was opened on the balcony overlooking the indoor pool so that members and guests no longer needed to change into street clothes for the old beverage lounge. In 1947, the bathers' bar was replaced with a Sand Bar at the north end of the clubhouse.

In the late 1940s and early 1950s, a brouhaha raged over the need for paddle tennis courts (and then more paddle tennis courts). One scheme after another was proposed, as frustrated beach club users faulted the board for lack of action. In 1949, $500 was allocated for such a construction, but rescinded in 1950. By 1964, the issue had still not been resolved, and the board voted to lease Santa Monica beach property for paddle tennis courts, but the City rejected the idea. In 1965, the plan was to build two paddle tennis courts on the land being used for the Club's parking.

In 1956, the Club announced plans to raze the Beach Facility, which "physically and functionally…leaves much to be desired." The ranch-style building planned by the Club would cost far less than rehabbing the old facility, according to A. L. Pozzo, the Club president. The indoor pool would be

eliminated, freeing up valuable space and a new pool would be constructed in the sand. Only two thirds of the old slab would be used, freeing up space for shuffleboard and paddle tennis courts.

Instead of destroying the old club, however, the board decided to enlarge and redesign the existing facility, spending $210,000. The green colored clubhouse was repainted adobe with black trim, and a gravel roof replaced a composition roof. A lowered ceiling was installed in the Lounge (now the Catalina Room) and a fireplace was added along the south wall, constructed out of bricks from the former dining room.

Ceiling-to-floor windows were installed along the ocean-view side of the building and the upper level was extended over the former sidewalk. A bar was installed next to the dining room.

The Jonathan Beach Club is within a year of the age of the Jonathan Town Club, yet it has been modified again and again to update it to current use. In 1959, a side entrance was added to make entry possible from the parking lot. Prior to that, guests entered from the highway side, through an entrance between the two stairways in the Catalina Room. In 1960, the front entrance was sealed off.

In 1967, the Club's architect, Earl Heitschmidt, proposed a structure with one level of parking below ground, one level at grade, and a roof used for four paddle tennis courts. This would cost a half-million dollars, would park 200 cars and would take eight months to complete. Heitschmidt presented an alternative to the vexing need for paddle tennis courts. Put them on the roof of the Club itself. This would mean redesigning and rebuilding the roof, but it could be finished in four months, would cost only $78,400 and would accommodate three courts.

For most of the Beach Club's years, the attire of members and guests was much more formal than it is today. In 1958, the house rules were redrafted to make clear that the upper level would "be available to only gentlemen in coats and ladies in dresses." In 1961, the Beach Club dress code was "further liberalized" to limit men's coats and women's dresses to Saturdays and special Club parties when dress is so designated, after 7 p.m.

Throughout this whole period, the future of the Beach Club was very much in question, because the state hadn't decided what form of expanded highway to build up the coast. Condemnation of the Club was a real possibility.

In 1965, the state had completed the Santa Monica Freeway to the coast and was now talking about how to bring the freeway north. A wide freeway that hugged the palisades would wipe out the Jonathan Club. If it was constructed as a causeway it would landlock the Club. Both the Santa Monica City Council and Chamber of Commerce favored an off-shore freeway/causeway because it would not divide Santa Monica, as an inland freeway would.

For years the Club was off balance, not knowing whether to invest in capital projects, find another club site, quit the Santa Monica coast or wait to see what developed.

The Beach Facility was under assault from both directions. The state was threatening from the highway side and Santa Monica was threatening from the surf side. In 1966, the City was demanding of beach front owners that they remove encroachments to a defined line, which, in the case of the Jonathan Club, was 190 feet oceanward from its roadside boundary. By 1967, the Club was in bad need of the repair that had been put off for years, waiting for word on government's plans.

The hunt was on for a new beach club. A committee was named "to study the possible acquisition of Westport Beach Club or merger with Westport Beach Club as well as the possibility of building a club on a new site." A yacht-mooring facility was also considered.

Also in 1967, the Club was having angst over the signal light situation. For many years the Club had lobbied to have a traffic signal installed adjacent to the Club entrance, but the signal light finally installed did not comply with regulations. So the number of traffic lanes was to be increased to seven (3+3+one lane for left turns driving south) and the California Incline was to be widened with a traffic island installed at Coast Highway. The plan was to prohibit left turns for northbound traffic and southbound traffic would be interrupted only when a pedestrian signaled to cross. The cost to the Club was significant. Ultimately a solution was found which allowed northbound and southbound access to the club at the signal light.

In 1968, the Club weighed the idea of a tie-in with "a good commercial hotel or motel, such as the Surf Rider, to the end that Jonathans would be given top preference for first class accommodations when needed," a suggestion which was later nixed.

Later in 1968, a novel idea was presented by the Dillingham Corporation: How about tearing down the existing Beach Facility and replacing it with an eight- to ten-story U-shaped building? The Jonathan Club would occupy the lower two floors on a 99-year lease for $1 a year, and condominiums for Jonathan Club members would fill the upper floors. An outdoor swimming pool and paddle tennis courts on the roof would enhance the project. The Jonathan Club board expressed unanimous interest in the scheme, but ultimately they rejected the Dillingham proposal and a similar offer from another developer. The board also rejected an offer from the Sand and Sea Club to purchase the Jonathan Beach Club.

In 1974, the State of California and the City of Santa Monica sued all of the property owners in Santa Monica along the beach, including the Jonathan Club, to establish the seaward boundaries of their properties. Following years of litigation the disputes were settled in 1983 with property owners agreeing to leases for portions of the properties in dispute. The Jonathan Club was able to keep using the part of its property that had been so important to its Beach Facility function.

In 1986, the major rooms of the Beach Facility were renamed. The Dining Room became the Pacific Room, the Old Card Room became the Sunset North and South, the Bar became the Palisades Lounge and the Main Lounge became the Catalina Room. In 1996, repairs and renovations were completed which included earthquake repairs, a steel and concrete bond beam around the circumference of the Beach Facility and three steel and concrete sheer walls the width and height of the Club. The Club was brought up to the standards of the Americans with Disabilities Act at the same time.

THE SEA BREEZE BEACH CLUB AND THE BEVERLY BEACH CLUB

The Jonathan Beach Club was their beach club first

The facility that is known today as the Jonathan Beach Club began its life in 1927 as the Sea Breeze Beach Club. It may come as a surprise to many Jonathan Club members that their functional, updated beach facility was opened only about a year after their ornate, formal Town Club. It may be a further surprise to learn that the Beach Facility, like the Town Club, was designed in the Italian Renaissance style.

In mid-1926, in the midst of the Santa Monica beach club boom, plans were announced for a beach club named Sea Breeze. The Sea Breeze Holding Company announced what it believed to be the largest lease transaction on record in Santa Monica, a 99-year lease totaling $3 million. A million dollars would be spent on building and furnishing the luxury club. The property, with its 285 feet of ocean front, was bought from C. L. and F. E. Bundy.

The architect was Gene Verge, who set the club back about 75 feet from the ocean. On the first floor of Verge's creation would be "an elaborately furnished lounge and lobby," a grill, beauty parlor, gentlemen's tonsorial parlor (barber shop) and "plunge room." On the mezzanine would be "the ladies' special dressing rooms." The second floor would feature a supper room and ballroom "of large proportions" and a nursery, "superintended by expert nurses."

The third floor was committed to recreational use and was virtually enclosed by glass. It contained card rooms, billiard rooms and rooms "for other diversions," according to the *Los Angeles Times*.

Among the board of governors members of the Sea Breeze Beach Club were Charles W. Lyon, State Senator; Pierson M. Hall, Councilman, Chairman, City Planning Committee; William I. Traeger, Sheriff, Los Angeles County; Jerry Mayer, Metro-Goldwin-Mayer Studios, Culver City; Eugene Biscailuz, Undersheriff, Los Angeles County; Willie Hunter, state golf champion, affiliated Brentwood Country Club; and Judge William H. Sheldon, a former member of the New York legislature. "Pioneer Life Members" of the Sea Breeze Club included actress Lillian Gish, Mrs. Jack Ford and Roscoe Arbuckle.

The Sea Breeze Beach Club opened on June 19, 1927, with a ten-day festival of water sport competitions which was open to the general public. By the time the club went under it had relaxed its rules to become a semi-public beach club. It advertised to visitors to the Los Angeles Olympic Games of 1932, offering "the same courtesies and the same prices that are given to [our] oldest and best customers." As that club was failing, a desperate member advertised in the *Los Angeles Times* offering to trade his membership for a radio.

In 1933, the defunct Sea Breeze Beach Club was bought by an organization headed by Thomas C. Bundy, a former tennis star, and perhaps a member of the same Bundy family that had held the Sea Breeze Club's lease. The Beverly Beach Club opened in June of 1933, promising that is was "not a promotion proposition" and that it would "own its own buildings, furniture and equipment, thereby permitting a small membership at a reasonable cost." It did not automatically accept those who'd been members of the Sea Breeze Beach Club, but put them through a new vetting process. This new Beverly Beach Club, heavy on tennis stars, was geared to a younger set, but it went under so quickly that the facility was still known to most people as the former Sea Breeze Beach Club.

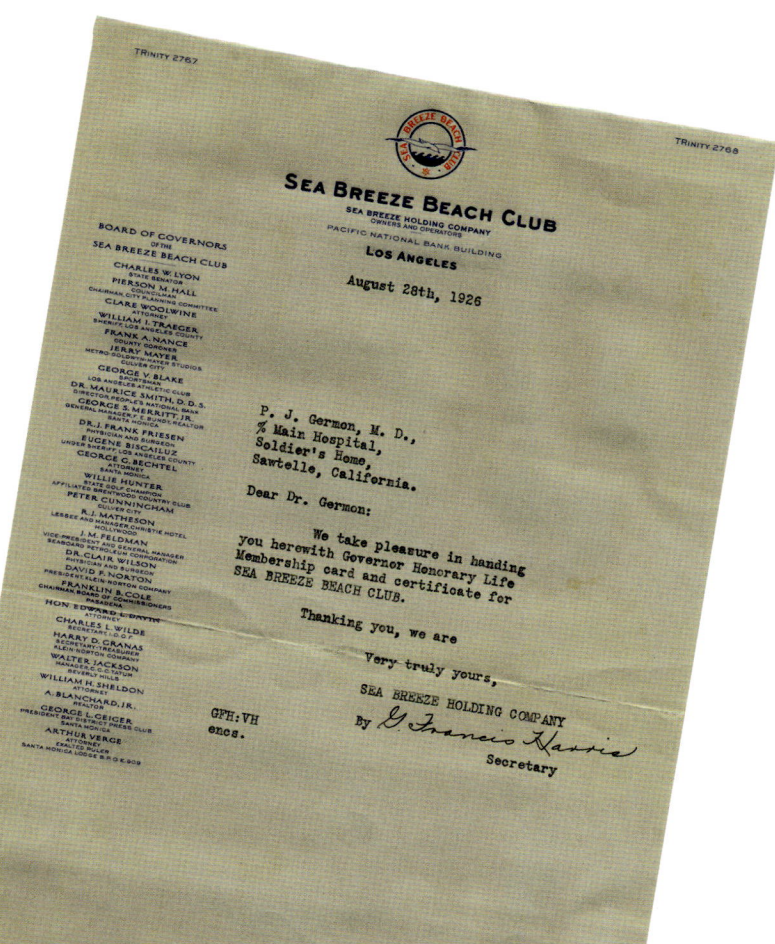

Chapter 7
War

Sgt. Bob Axelrod named an Army half-track after the Club in the European campaign in World War II. The mobile fortress "The Jonathan Club" saw "lively action prior to the German surrender." Sgt. Axelrod, a former Jonathan Club assistant manager and Maitre D', is shown with the gunnery crew pointing to aircraft.

IF IT'S NOT A DEPRESSION IT'S A WAR!

The Club rebounds in the 1940s

War broke out in Europe in 1939, and America braced for possible war across both oceans, waking the Sleeping Beauty of a booming economy from a ten-year slumber. By 1939, the Club was able to put money into a building that had had no capital improvements in the 14 years since its construction, but each repair and rehabilitation had to be approved by Pacific Mutual Insurance Company. The nightmare of the Depression was over but the storm of a world war was on the horizon. Prices of Club services began to rise again.

LeRoy Edwards had served the Club as its president from 1933 until 1937 and had saved the Club at the nadir of the Depression. He was succeeded by another attorney, Louis Canepa, who led the Club during the remainder of the Depression and through the World War II years. Canepa had been on the Board since 1932, during the Jeffries years. Like Jeffries, his was a forceful leadership style, and like Jeffries, he perpetuated a loyal board year after year with almost no change in the Club's leadership team.

On April 9, 1941, the Club granted Honorary Military Suspensions for Marion Flay Baugh and four other members who were part of America's military buildup. By summer the Club had offered three-month memberships to all U.S. commissioned officers stationed in Southern California, for $3.00 a month. Commanders of large units in the area temporarily were allowed to designate officers of their commands for visitor's cards. Towards the end of the war the Club established quotas for different ranks in the service. In December, 1944, the quotas for military ranks O-3 and below were closed.

After the attack on Pearl Harbor on December 7, 1941, the board began to think about stockpiling canned food. The board formed a secret committee, with board member and National Guard Colonel Andrew Copp as its chairman, to "scrutinize employees of the club regarding alien or other United States Government enemies and report back to the Board." On January 3, less than a month after Pearl Harbor, the Club lost its first member to the war, Marion Flay

- 1940 – Los Angeles population: 1,504,277
- 1940 – Freeways debut in the West with Arroyo Parkway (Pasadena Freeway)
- 1940 – Second floor Town Club bar installed where men's room is today
- 1940 – Lunch counter installed in Grill Room for those in a hurry
- 1941 – Air conditioning of Town Club begins
- 1941 – U.S. enters World War II after December 7 Pearl Harbor attack
- 1944 – 13th Floor dining room named the Cape Cod Room
- 1945 – World War II ends

Baugh, who died in a plane crash in China while serving as a flight instructor for Claire Chennault's Flying Tigers.

In 1942, an ever-growing number of Jonathans put on the uniforms of their country to serve in the war effort, including one board member, Col. Andrew J. Copp, Jr., who was ordered to active duty in Washington, D.C. He remained on the board throughout his active duty, participating by mail. By the end of the war, at least 237 members of the Club had served in the Armed Forces.

Rooms in the Town Club were used for officers of all branches of the service going and coming to various theaters of the war. The Town Club swimming pool was used for swimming instructions for military personnel, mostly officers.

The restrictions of a nation at war impacted the Club. The board discussed allowing its facilities to be designated as an air raid shelter, but ultimately this was not done. Room service and staffing of special rooms was discontinued because of War Manpower Commission regulations, "except where there is illness." A War Savings Bond Committee solicited members with considerable success. Members who ate all of their meals in the clubhouse were encouraged to give their ration cards to the Club.

Because of meat rationing, members sometimes brought their own meat to the Club to be cooked for their guests, receiving a discount for their meals as a result. Later in the war no meat was served on Tuesdays or Fridays even if the member wanted to bring his own meat. Only one pat of butter per meal was served to each diner. Members were limited to the purchase of one bottle of liquor per week from the Club.

Provisions were made at the Club for periods of "black-outs" when the threat of attack mandated that no lights be visible in the city. In those cases blackout curtains were pulled over the windows of the Main Dining Room, Grill Room and other inside quarters to darken the Club from the outside. The entire Seventh Floor was cleared as overnight accommodations for members and their families who happened to be at the Club at the time and could not return home.

After the war returning Club servicemen were guaranteed a room at the club, if they so desired. The Club voted Honorary Memberships to General Dwight D. Eisenhower, Admiral Chester Nimitz (a former member when Commander of the Pacific Fleet), President Harry S Truman, Captain E. V. Rickenbacher, and renewed the Honorary Membership status of General George C. Marshall,

One might say that World War II ended for the Jonathan Club on October 1, 1946, when all members on Honorary Military Suspension status were transferred back to their regular Club status.

Honorary member Arthur Beaumont, said to be the most distinguised naval artist of World War II, rendered this watercolor of the USS James C. Owens, a destroyer escort named for a Jonathan Club member who was a hero of the Battle of Midway. Beaumont created the work of art for the hero's father, James C. Owens, Sr., also a Jonathan Club member.

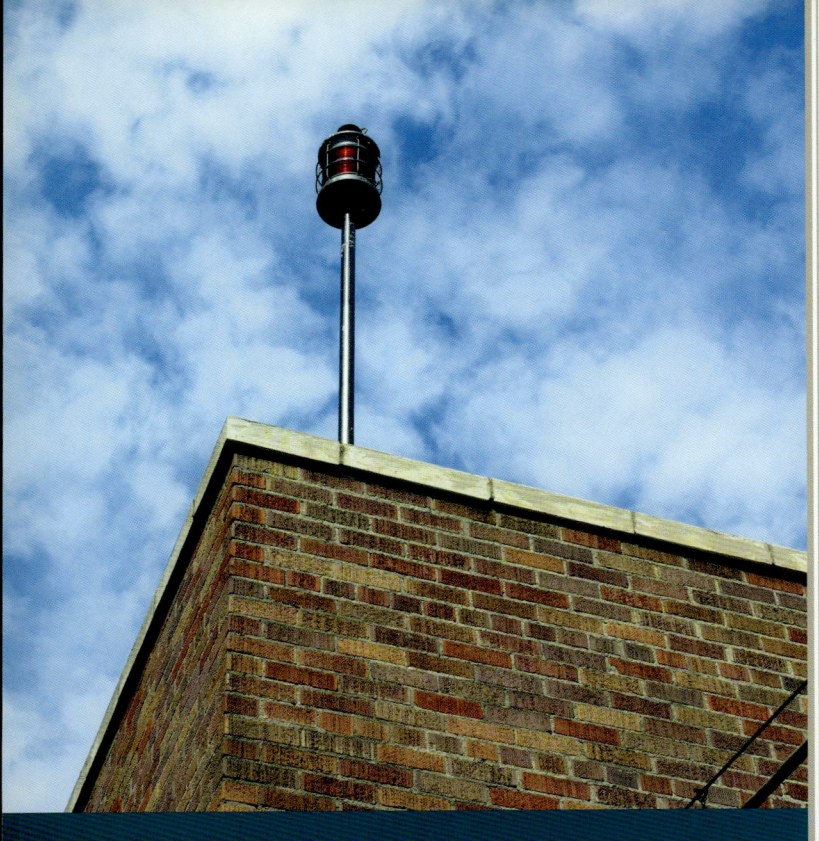

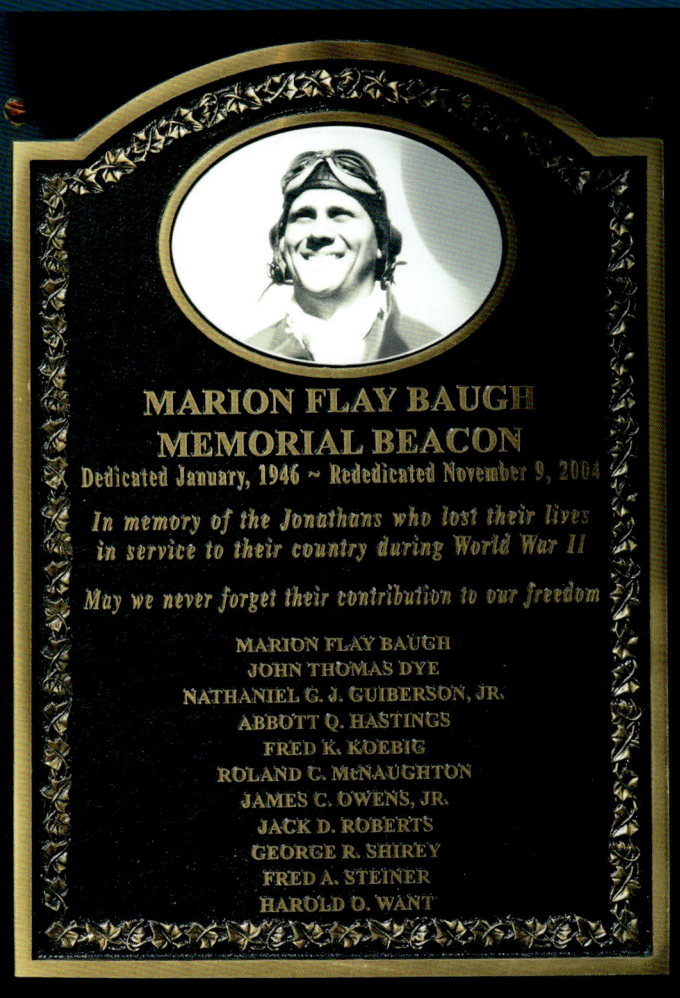

Marion Flay Baugh Memorial Beacon

In December, 1945, the Club recognized the Club members who had died in World War II with a unique memorial. The Jonathan Town Club was one of the tallest buildings in the City at that time, and aircraft had come of age in the war just ended. So the Club erected a flashing red aircraft beacon on top of the Club. It was a mournful signal visible from Pasadena, Long Beach and Santa Monica, and a hopeful signal to guide errant sprits back to their Club home. The Club named the light for the first of the Jonathan Club members to die in the war…a pilot…as the Marion Flay Baugh Memorial Beacon.

The light was dedicated to the eight Jonathan Club members known to have died in the war. There were at that time three Jonathans in the status of Missing in Action. It was too early to tell whether they may have been prisoners of war and might still somehow be alive, so the Club went ahead and dedicated the light to the eight known dead with the promise that as soon as the status of the missing three could be determined, more names would be added if appropriate.

It was a promise not kept. The Jonathans went about rebuilding their lives after the Great Depression and the Great War and forgot about the three Jonathans unaccounted for. In the 1960s and 1970s, high-rise buildings created a wall around the Jonathan Club blocking the suburbs' view of the light, which, over the years, fell out of repair and burned out. In 1995, the Centennial Committee reminded the Club of that long-forgotten beacon, had it put back in working order and placed a small remembrance below it. That remembrance, however, still listed only the original eight. In 2004, the oversight was corrected with a ceremony and the addition of the three members listedin 1945 as Missing in Action but later declared to have died in the war.

Even so, the commemoration was not complete. A few other Jonathans died in World War II, but were somehow overlooked when the list was compiled in 1945. As this book is written a war memorial is being planned for the Town Club Lobby, which will list all known members and dependents who died in uniform during all periods of U.S. war.

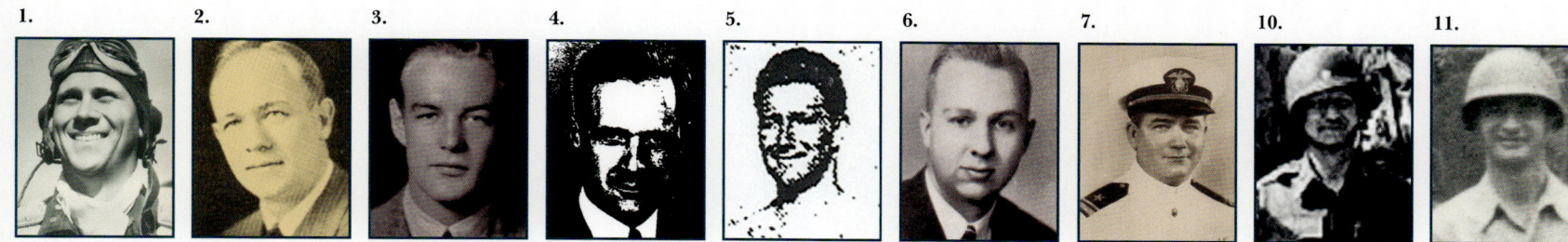

The eleven Jonathan Club members honored by the Marion Flay Baugh Memorial Beacon are:

1. Marion Flay Baugh
Marion Flay Baugh, former Army Air Forces 1Lt., was one of 80 pilots in the famous Flying Tigers, and his plane went down in China only a few weeks after Pearl Harbor. He was the fourth Flying Tiger to die during their campaign in China, killed when his plane crashed near Kunming, China, while transporting a radio operator.

2. John Thomas Dye
Navy Lt. John Thomas Dye III was the executive officer of a destroyer escort, USS *Underhill*, when the ship encountered a group of kaiten, midget suicide submarines, between Okinawa and the Philippines. The ship rammed one of the subs, which exploded its torpedo, sinking the American ship and killing Lt. Dye on July 24, 1945.

3. Nathaniel G. Guiberson, Jr.
Army Air Forces 1Lt. Nathaniel G. Guiberson, Jr., flew with the 370th Bomb Squadron of the 307th Heavy Bomb Group. His plane went down in the seas near the Philippine Islands. His crew was seen leaving the aircraft in a life raft and an enemy plane was seen strafing the men. The search for the crew was called off after five days.

4. Abbott Q. Hastings
Navy Lt. Abbott Quincy Hastings was a technical observer on a patrol aircraft based in Hawaii. Somewhere between Hawaii and the mainland United States, his plane went down on March 4, 1944. He is commemorated in the National Cemetery in Honolulu.

5. Fred J. Koebig
Army Air Forces Maj. Fred J. Koebig, 1940 Student Body President of UCLA for the Class of 1940, was in Hawaii during the December 7, 1941, attack itself. Rising quickly to the rank of Major, his bomber went down and he was captured and held prisoner on Rabaul Island, where he was executed on March 5, 1944.

6. Roland McNaughton
Army Air Forces Capt. Roland C. McNaughton was one of twelve chosen in October, 1941, to train the native army of the Philippines. He was captured in May of 1942 after the fall of Bataan and Corregidor. He was among 1,600 officers aboard a Japanese ship which was sunk by American forces on December 13, 1944.

7. James C. Owens, Jr.
Navy Lt. James C. Owens, Jr., a pilot with Torpedo Squadron 8 aboard USS *Hornet* (CV-8), died early in the Battle of Midway. Although every plane in the squadron was shot down, their attack stripped away enemy air cover and made ultimate American victory possible. Destroyer Escort USS *James C. Owens* (DE-776) was named in his honor.

8. Jack D. Roberts (No photo available)
Navy Lt. Jack D. Roberts was the aide to Coast Guard Capt. L. M. Harding, who led the effort to develop the navigational system Loran during the war. Lt. Roberts reached Iceland, the Faeroe Islands and the Hebrides, remote and dangerous sites. Lt. Roberts died on July 31, 1944, when his plane went down in the Pacific.

9. George Shirey (No photo available)
Army Air Forces Aviation Cadet George Russell Shirey was killed in an airplane crash near Gardner Field, in Taft, with his flight instructor on June 7, 1943, while in training.

10. Fred A. Steiner
Army Lt. Col. Fred Steiner was the executive officer of the 8th Infantry Regiment of the 4th Infantry Division which hit the famous Utah Beach on Normandy on D-Day. Col. Steiner led the attack on Montebourg a few days later. A week after D-Day, on June 12, 1944, while escorting Brig. Gen. Theodore Roosevelt, son of the former president, he was killed by a sniper.

11. Harold O. Want
Army Sgt. Hal Want, Signal Corps, came ashore in France and marched across Europe. In Germany in the Spring of 1944, ahead of the main American forces, he stumbled across Germans retreating in their armed vehicle. Want was badly injured in the mismatch and died in England a year later on April 13, 1945.

LOUIS CANEPA SELLS THE BEACH FACILITY AND LOSES HIS OFFICE

Two Jonathan Club presidents have been removed from office in the middle of their elected terms. William Jeffries was removed in 1930 for buying the Beach Facility. In the late 1940s, Louis Canepa was removed for trying to sell it.

Louis Canepa had been president of the Club for eight years by 1945, and his power had been almost absolute. He had given immense amounts of time to the Club, and he and his board had been returned to office year after year. On March 14, 1945, Canepa and his board sold the Beach Facility. They didn't *propose* selling it. They *sold* it.

They accepted an offer of $125,000 subject to "(a) The ability of the Club to convey a title satisfactory to grantee, (b) Transfer of two on sale liquor licenses to grantee or his nominee at the same time and (c) Such approval of the membership as the Board of Directors shall deem sufficient." The sale went into a 60-day escrow immediately. Over a month went by before the board bothered to share this action with the membership. A letter to members was approved by the board on April 23. The response was immediate. A group of members invoked their right to call a special meeting.

The special meeting of the membership was held in the gym of the Town Club on May 2, followed quickly by two more special meetings on May 7 and May 10. Some 356 members showed up on Thursday, May 10, "to discuss proposed sale of the Jonathan Swimming Club at Santa Monica." When the vote was taken the members were unanimous: The Beach Facility should not be sold.

The following Monday, the board dutifully cancelled the escrow, and returned the deposit of $25,000 to the buyer.

The matter was far from over. The membership, which had for so long been comfortable with the Club leadership, and had not paid the governance much attention, had now bolted wide awake.

That Monday happened also to be the day of the annual meeting and election. Canepa had listed the four present board members who were to be dutifully reelected at the pro forma election, but this year it was different. An alternate slate was offered and the challengers were swept into office. The board now had five old members and four new members, Squire

Johnson, Charles Pritchard, C. J. Turner and Joseph Spray. The new members attempted to displace Canepa with Squire Johnson, saying "The incidents immediately preceding the last election, and the exceedingly large vote at the election is…a clear expression of disapproval of the administration policies of the past of all directors, rather than the repudiation of the four members of the Board who were defeated. The powers of the presidency have rested in the same hands for the past eight years. Now we have a clear mandate from the membership for a change." Predictably, the five old members kept Canepa in office.

The new board members disputed the way the number of board seats had been settled on. Did the bylaws and the actions taken by the membership in years past indicate that there be seven, nine or eleven directors? Ultimately it was decided that the board should be increased from nine to eleven.

At a special meeting of the membership on October 22, 1946, in a whirlwind of resignations and elections, a new board of eleven was constituted. Louis Canepa was still president.

This new board now turned its energy on a subject which the old board had always blocked. The board challenged the expenses that President Canepa and Secretary Joseph J. Malone had charged to the club, and the accounting firm hired by the board, Ernst & Ernst, found irregularities. Canepa and Malone stubbornly held on to their jobs, despite calls for their resignation, promising to step down at some later date. Their time ran out on March 27, 1947, when both of the men resigned from their posts and from the board.

On April 18, 1947, at yet another special membership meeting, Judge Beno Brink succeeded in a motion that forbade the newly elected board from taking any action against Canepa and Malone for the irregularities that Ernst & Ernst had found.

At that meeting the members also voted to vest the power to make and amend bylaws in the members and not the board to avoid the controversy over board composition that the Club had just struggled through.

It wasn't long before the Club changed the bylaws to limit directors to three-year terms and limit presidents to a single year to avoid the kinds of entrenched, ongoing regimes that Jeffries and Canepa had represented.

Chapter 8
RECENT TIMES

Postwar years: Much energy and potential mischief

The years of the 1950s, and especially the 1960s, were times of tremendous energy within the Jonathan Club. In retrospect, entirely too much energy at times. It was a period of restlessness after decades of depression and war. In the 1920s, the Town Club was still too new for change. In the 1930s, there had been no money to change either the Town Club or Beach Facility. In the 1940s, there were war-related shortages that discouraged change. Suddenly, in the 1950s and 1960s, there was a booming economy, plenty of materials and two facilities that were too old to be appealing and not old enough to be thought of as historic or precious.

Boards during this period seriously considered tearing down both facilities. In 1955, the board decided that, as the Club sold off property, members should be notified so they could submit bids. The dowdy old 1920s Italian Renaissance building was sadly out of step with the dazzling steel-and-glass wonders filling the skyline and Los Angeles had finally raised the decades-old 150-foot height limit, leaving the Town Club discouraging close to earth. The country was replacing Old World artistry and embellishment as fast as contractors and interior designers could be hired. Solid paneling replaced wainscoting, wall-to-wall carpeting replaced wood and marble floors, lighting of simple design replaced ornate chandeliers, and drop ceilings became necessary to buffer the new air conditioning, which had turned the corner from luxury to necessity. Acoustic tile was slapped on any downward-facing surface as if the arms race with the Soviets was to be won by whoever applied it in the greatest quantity. This was also the era when elevator operators were displaced with do-it-yourself buttons.

It was good to be able to make investments in the Club's two facilities after such a financial drought, but the first aid almost killed both patients.

Membership stood at high, healthy levels, and the usage of the Town Club was dramatized by the nightly crowd, packed three deep, along the full 49-foot-five-inch length of the Tap Room bar, with so many patrons that drinks for the outer ring had to be passed over the heads of those closer to the bar. In 1958, the board declared that it had no intention of aggressively seeking new members because the Town Club facilities were overcrowded at lunchtime as it was.

But where were the fast-changing times taking society and where were they taking the Jonathan Club? A December 24, 1958, *The Wall Street Journal* article examined the fate of private clubs. It pointed out that the suburbanization of America was replacing town clubs with country clubs. And the democratization of social values and the growing popularity of outdoor activities were eroding the niche that town clubs had played for the better part of a century. All this at a time when total expenses of town clubs had risen nine percent in the past five years and payroll costs had risen 25 percent over the past five years.

A letter from Jonathan Club member Charles W. Horn to the Club's president in January, 1959, sobered the board. He wrote, "If as many believe, few private town clubs are likely to prosper in the years ahead, the Jonathan Club may be entering a period of fiscal decline of challenging dimensions." He warned that the Club was "anchored too firmly in the traditions of the past." He wrote that he had talked to a number of "eligible prospects" who contended that they did not "need" a town club. "A country club, yes. A Beach Club, no." These prospects were asking rhetorically, "Why pay $1200.00 and $31.50 a month for the privilege of eating and drinking occasionally?" Horn wrote "Our 'competition' is not so much Other Clubs. As a town club the Jonathan excels in every category of service and accommodations. Our competition lies largely in the areas of today's fast-changing economic, social, cultural and business complex." He summed up his assessment with a conclusion, "I know our patient isn't on his death-bed. But there is no question he is showing symptoms of malnutrition, if not malpractice....the whole puzzle is to be solved in the answer to this simple, albeit profound question: 'WHO REALLY NEEDS THE CLUB – AND WHY?'"

1950s

The postwar construction of freeways affected both facilities. As the 1950s began, the state announced that it would be constructing the Harbor Freeway just west of the Town Club and that a major off-ramp would change the urban landscape around the building, and make the parking entrance off Sixth Street unusable. The Club's architects made changes along the south side of the Town Club accordingly.

Late in 1950, an "Improvement Fund" was established by tacking $5.00 a month onto each member's dues. With this fund the Club bought the Carlton Hotel property to the north of the Town Club and two small parcels immediately to the southwest and northwest of the Town Club so that the Jonathan Club now occupied the entire southern half of the block. The Improvement Fund also paid for an addition to the parking garage, renewed the building's plumbing and extensively renovated all of the Town Club's major spaces.

The addition to the parking garage added a basement level and two above-ground stories to accommodate 400 more cars in the club. "No longer will the ladies in evening attire have to walk through the garage and down the stairs to reach the entrance, as was necessary under the old facilities," said the September 1953 issue of *The Jonathan*. Although the initial architect's renderings show a continuation of the 1925 Town Club stone exterior, the final design was the karma of the 50s running over the dogma of the 20s. (In 1970 three more stories were added to the garage, elongating the vertical slashes of the 50s design, and passing up an opportunity to blend with the 1925 Town Club a second time.)

1960s

The mood of the times showed through with discussions of using the garage basement as a fallout shelter. The Watts riots had caused a number of cancellations for the annual Del Mar Day. These were troubling times. In 1964, the board authorized the fitting out of a first-aid-hospital equipped room at the Club.

Perhaps the most significant achievements of the Club in the 1960s were what it didn't do. In 1966, the board had plans prepared to take 1,000 feet from the Reading Room with an entrance to the Town Club through the Second Floor. The board also considered selling its garage to a developer who would construct a monstrous, 2,800-car parking structure, with three floors below grade and four floors above, stretching from the Jonathan Club to Fifth Street, with spaces dedicated to the Club.

In 1967, as plans were developed for the skyscraping towers of Atlantic Richfield across Figueroa from the Club, the board began to explore selling the Town Club to a developer who would raze it and build another central city high rise. The Jonathan Club could then take space in one of the upper floors of the Atlantic Richfield Towers.

Ladies' Christmas party, 1958

A company "of national importance" sought to buy the Jonathan Club in 1968, raze the clubhouse, build a 55-story tower and install a Club in its upper floors. The board politely declined, but it kept on debating the similar offer from Atlantic Richfield. A study by the architectural firm of Albert C. Martin & Associates estimated that the cost of a new club would be about $9 million.

The board was so serious about selling the Town Club that it asked the real estate firm of Cushman & Wakefield "for a specific proposal which would include information as to air rights and other details."

In 1960, the Club had come very close to selling the Beach Club. And, in 1967, the board had appointed a special committee "to study the possible acquisition of another beach club, a merger, or building on a new site." Now, in 1968, at the same time the board was discussing selling the Town Club for demolition, it expressed interested in a suggestion by Dillingham Corporation to "acquire the Beach Club property and build an eight to ten story 'U'-shaped building on the property. The first two floors would be devoted to Club use, the upper levels to be condominiums for Jonathans only. The project would include an outdoor swimming pool and subterranean parking. The facility would be erected at no expense to the Jonathan Club and leased to the Club for a 99 year period at a dollar a year. Paddle tennis courts would be installed on the roof."

The years of 1968 and 1969 formed one of the most tumultuous periods in American history, with the Vietnam War protests, the Woodstock music festival, the assassination of Rev. Martin Luther King, Jr., and Senator Robert Kennedy and the human race's first step on the Moon. Meanwhile, the Club was going through its own upheaval. As the board wrestled with whether to sell its two real estate stakes, it pondered such 1960s questions as protecting the Town Club in a riot "in view of the current social unrest and increasing threat of riot or raids by marauding bands," whether to build "an intimate cocktail lounge" somewhere in the Club and whether to allow turtle-neck sweaters at black-tie events.

Finally, on March 25, 1969, the board had made up its mind about the Town Club. It would keep its present facility, thank you very much. But the decisions which seem so logical today had been reached after great debate by the Club's board of directors. By the end of 1969, and the end of a turbulent decade, the board seems also to have decided not to tear down the Beach Facility.

The Ladies' Elevator is now permanently out of service.

1970s AND 1980s AND BEYOND

The times they are a-changin'

As one reads the board minutes of the 1970s and 1980s one can almost hear Bob Dylan wailing, "The Times They Are A-Changin'." The creaky old premises of inclusion and exclusion were under growing attack. So were dress codes that had stood unchallenged for so many decades. As the role of women changed in society the tide of social change rose higher and higher around the castle tower until it poured over the top of the battlements. By the end of the 1980s, the waves of social change had so completely swept over the Club that the old footprints were invisible and forgotten.

The double decade of the 1970s and 1980s might be thought of as the decline of the post-World War II era. The late 1940s, the 1950s and most of the 1960s had been absorbed with rebuilding an infrastructure rusty from the Depression and starved by wartime shortages, in which classical decoration was replaced with simple Bauhaus lines. In 1970, the Town Club Lobby was stripped of its Italian Renaissance grandeur. The Club president at the time, Jarl Nerdrum, beamed, "Giving the lobby a thorough facelifting eliminates a very unfavorable first impression of the Club without trading the traditional décor for out-of-place chrome and glass." By the end of the 1980s, society, and the Club, better appreciated the art of former times, and the Jonathan Club had restored its Lobby to a semblance of its old glory.

The dawn of the 1970s was an extension of the tumultuous 1960s, and Jonathan Club members struggled with the sight of men with shoulder length hair in the dining rooms. And what was to be done about women wearing pants? In 1978, the board voted to allow pantsuits in good taste, but went back to a skirts-only rule for almost a decade before allowing pants permanently. The growing number of men in more casual attire seeking to eat in the Tap Room were banished to the Fifth Floor to be served their cocktails by room service. By October of 1972 the Club had radically relaxed its dress code to allow men in proper jackets to come to the Tap Room without ties for pre- and post-game events.

But the force that most changed the Club in the 1970s and 1980s was society's growing impatience with ethnic and gender discrimination. At the beginning of 1970 all the historic Club barriers were firmly in place; by 1989 there was not a splinter remaining. Chip by chip by chip the solid wall was pecked away. The Ladies door on Figueroa was closed in December of 1970 and men were allowed to accompany women in the Ladies' Elevator in 1971. In 1974, women were allowed in the Lobby (at first only in the evenings) and then in the main elevators. In 1975 women were allowed to stay overnight at the Club with their husbands in guest rooms (at first only after major club events).

The U.S. Equal Opportunity Employment Commission began hounding the Club in 1972, and in 1974 the Hospitality Committee and House Committee suggested to the board that women be admitted as members. Pressure built within the membership and within the board itself. But it would take lawsuits from government bodies, the ebbing of the old membership and the growing of a younger membership before the old barriers were finally dismantled, in 1987, and the last male bastion in the Club, the Second Floor, was opened to women in 1989, as the two-decade era of change drew to a close.

The Beach Facility began year-round operations in 1971. Meanwhile, as the downtown Los Angeles skyline grew around the Town Club, the board wrestled with whether to sell the air rights. City codes allowed a developer to extend a building above the normal height limit by buying the air rights of another building. With only 13 stories, the Jonathan Club was a logical seller and the price would be well over a million dollars. On the one hand it seemed unlikely that the Club would ever add to the height of its historic building, but on the other hand, selling the air rights would handicap future boards forever. In the end the Club decided not to sell the air rights, and the law allowing such exchanges later changed, so the question is now moot. Another influence of the development of the time was the fascination with condominium use of buildings. The Club considered condos at both the Town Club and Beach Facility, but ultimately ruled against both possibilities.

The decades of the 1970s and 1980s had begun as relatively quiet times for the Jonathan Club and by the end of 1989 were subdued once again. The 1990s saw a financially stable club and a decade of capital renovation. The centennial celebration of the Club, in 1995, was an event which filled rooms from the Lobby to the roof of the Town Club and was probably the most extravagant event in the Club's history. To prepare for that night members were dunned a token amount for a period leading up to the anniversary. Each member received a Centennial book about the Club's history at the 100th anniversary celebration.

Since the early 1960s, the Club struggled with what to do with the vacant Eigth and Ninth Floors. That debate was taken up by one board of directors after another and continue through the rest of the century before the unused floors were finally converted to luxury overnight suites in 2003.

Also in the new century the Staples Center was opened, and with it a Jonathan Club suite. This introduced the evening ritual of shuttling Club members and guests in both directions, to sporting and concert events at Staples a few blocks to the south and to cultural events in the Music Center a few blocks to the north.

A leaf is turned – into a model club

A generation ago – in the mid-1980s – the Jonathan Club changed its membership process to one that was not based on gender, race or religion. Sixty-four percent of today's Jonathan Club members have come into the Club since that time and have never known first-hand the policies of discrimination that came before. In that respect it is not their grandfather's club.

Ethnic, religious and gender discrimination among private clubs was virtually universal across the face of America prior to the late 1980s. It was certainly true in the Jonathan Club. But the Jonathan Club was probably no better and no worse than similar clubs of the time. Nor was the bias in America's clubs limited to expensive, exclusive town, beach and country clubs. Every Rotary, Kiwanis and Lions Club in every large city and every tiny village, in every state of the union, was, by its charter, a male-only bastion until the same year that rules were changed in the Jonathan Club. And most of those service clubs, until at least the late 1960s, and often the 70s or 80s, excluded non-white ethnicities as well.

So, the Jonathan Club story, as painful as it is, is little different than those of other private clubs. Private clubs are the social caboose of our society, the very last to arrive at the boundary of any social trend, whether it is casual dress on Fridays, indoor baseball caps, bare midriffs, cell phones or membership policy changes.

Max Vorspan and Lloyd P. Gartner, in their *History of the Jews of Los Angeles*, described how early clubs in Los Angeles included Jewish members, but that the pattern changed over the years. They describe extensive Jewish participation in the dedication of the Los Angeles Athletic Club's first building and how, among the exclusive first 150 members of the California Club, at least twelve were Jewish. The Jonathan Club's early rolls included very prominent Jewish members, among which were the Hellman banking family. In 1930, in a good natured promotion of a club event, *The Jonathan* magazine included blurbs by an Italian and a Jewish member describing the event in Italian and Yiddish text. As authors Vorspan and Gartner document, this pattern of Jewish inclusion changed from the 1930s through the 1980s. The Jonathan Club probably always had Jewish members throughout its history, but during its middle years those members were admitted very selectively. That element of the Club's discrimination collapsed without notice as the public spotlight was directed to women and African Americans.

Exclusion of non-white ethnicities was more absolute. African Americans were not included as members or guests at the Jonathan Club prior to a policy reversal in the mid-1980s.

The club histories of the top clubs throughout the country reflect similar stories: pressure for change from both within and without beginning in the late 1960s, growing in the 1970s and succeeding around 1987. Legal action played a role in the changes at the Jonathan Club. The action came on two fronts, from the City of Santa Monica and the State Coastal Commission because of the Club's public beach frontage, and, at the Town Club, from the City of Los Angeles because of that city's anti-discrimination law.

Some Santa Monica City Council members in the 1970s and 1980s were openly hostile to the Jonathan Club because of its membership and guest practices. In 1985, the State Coastal Commission ordered the Club to adopt a non-discriminatory policy before it would be allowed to use state-owned land for parking and paddle tennis courts. The Commission's decision was ultimately upheld by the State Supreme Court and then the U.S. Supreme Court.

The first instance of a woman to be formally proposed and officially turned down came in September of 1977. Other women sought to be proposed into the mid-1980s, but somehow the Club found deficiencies in each individual candidate, protesting that their rejection had nothing to do with their gender and that the Club's charter did not specifically exclude anyone. So a circle of powerful downtown women began to assemble a group of highly qualified female executives and professionals to have their proposals considered at one time. They theorized that the Club would be forced to accept the group – or many in it – because it couldn't pretend to find non-gender reasons for turning down so many candidates with such high qualifications. While the women were putting this strategy together in 1987 the Club began to admit women.

Minorities were admitted before women. In early 1987, the Jonathan Club admitted its first African American members. The first of these was a senior executive of the Disney organization, Dennis F. Hightower. The Club mailed a questionnaire to its members in April, 1987, asking whether women should be admitted. Eighty percent said yes, and the Club made plans to admit women to membership.

The board decided to first give Widow Members the first option at full Resident Membership. The first of the women in Widow status to pay the difference in initiation fee and be accepted as a Resident Member was Louise M. Fitzgerald. The first woman admitted from the outside to full membership in the Jonathan Club was Brooke Knapp, owner of a private investment company and celebrated aviator. The California Club admitted its first woman to membership the following year.

Even after women were admitted to the Club, their dues were discounted by $15 because the Second Floor, including the Grill Room, Tap Room and Library, was still male-only. In 1988, Los Angeles City Attorney Jim Hahn targeted this last male refuge within the Jonathan Club. The Jonathan Club, meanwhile, sued the City in Federal Court challenging the constitutionality of its ordinance. By June of the following year even the sacred Second Floor was open to women and Los Angeles City Attorney Hahn dropped his suit against the Jonathan Club.

On May 24, 1988, the Los Angeles City Council passed an ordinance banning discrimination on the basis of sex, race, color, religion, ancestry or national origin. The ordinance applied only to private clubs with over 400 members and was clearly aimed at the Jonathan and California Clubs. The following month the U.S. Supreme Court weighed in, validating a law in New York that was nearly identical to that of Los Angeles, allowing cities to force large, exclusive private clubs to admit women and minorities. By this time, of course, the Jonathan Club's membership rolls were already sprinkled with women and minorities.

As this book is written a woman is president of the Jonathan Club and a woman is chair of the committee that oversees the Library on the formerly male-only Second Floor sanctuary. For almost two thirds of the current members of the Jonathan Club what they know of past membership discrimination cannot come from personal experience because they never belonged to that Jonathan Club.

Chapter 9
ART

GREAT CLUBS HAVE GREAT ART

Art became important to the Club when it moved into its grand quarters in the Pacific Electric Building, in 1905. Art and a bit of sculpture had adorned the prior headquarters at 132 South Spring Street, but no art that we know of from the Spring Street days survives in today's Club quarters.

Some of the art that distinguished the 1905 clubhouse atop the Pacific Electric Building does survive in today's Town Club. The large sculpture in the 1905 lobby, "The Combatants" by Cattalucci, was the theme piece for the Club. It guards the south end of the Town Club swimming pool today. Large Chinese metal vases from the 1905 Club stand as sentinels to the stacks in today's Town Club library, a century later. A statue of Napoleon that the Club bought in 1907, for $500, is still on display. The art of The Jonathan Club in the Pacific Electric Building included paintings and sculpture, and was overseen by an Art Committee that included Henry Edwards Huntington. The art of the early Jonathan Club reflected the American preference in that era for European art.

Huntington lent various art works to the Club for display but there is no record of his making gifts of art to The Jonathan Club.

The heart of today's Town Club art collection is paintings of the plein air California Impressionist school. The first of these paintings still held in the Club's current collection was "California Landscape," by Granville Redmond, which the Club bought for $500, in 1905, when the legendary Redmond was 34 years old. The painting had been accepted for exhibitions in the art building at the St. Louis World's Fair the year before. The Club purchased a "marine view" by Redmond the same year for $100, but this was possibly the "Marine Oil Painting" which was stolen in 1917.

In 1915, a painting entitled "Mount Shasta" was purchased for $275 from "the Administrator of the De Baker Estate." This is possibly the large "Mount Shasta" painting by William Keith which hangs in the Town Club's Florentine Lounge today. If so, the purchase of this 1879 painting would have come four years after the artist's death.

With the move into new quarters at Sixth and Figueroa Streets, the Club established the new membership category of Artists' Life Membership, through which "any artist otherwise eligible for Club membership, may become a Life Member, on presentation of one of his own paintings to the Club, subject to approval by Board and Art Committee, and in their opinion valued at not less than $1,000." The number of such artists was to be limited at any one time to ten. Such artists were to have all of the privileges of an Active Member. The first artist to hold this distinction was Jack Wilkinson Smith, Member Number A-1. Smith (1873-1949) had studied in the Art Institute of Chicago, was a staff artist with the *Cincinnati Enquirer* and earned national fame with his sketches from the front lines during the Spanish-American War. He moved to California in 1906 and distinguished himself as a founder of the California Art Club and leading member of the Laguna Beach art colony. He is regarded as one of California's most important painters, known for his Sierra landscapes, missions and marines. Two of his marine paintings hang in the Town Club Lobby, one over the fireplace and one over the concierge desk. Another of Smith's marines hangs in the Florentine Lounge and a high sierra painting of a mountain glacier with snow in moonlight hangs in the Third Floor Hall.

Granville Redmond (1871 – 1935) *California Landscape (Oaks And Meadows)*
Oil on canvas, Jonathan Club #687

Redmond was born in Philadelphia and came to California with his family in 1874. A victim of scarlet fever, which left him deaf at the age of two, he was enrolled in 1879 in the Institution for the Deaf, Dumb, and Blind at Berkeley (now called the California School for the Deaf, in Fremont). He attended the California School of Design, then studied at the Académie Julian in Paris and returned to California. After stints in Laguna Beach, Long Beach, Catalina Island, San Pedro, the Monterey Peninsula and San Mateo he settled in Los Angeles with dreams of using his pantomime skills in silent movies. Charlie Chaplin gave him a minor role in "A Dog's Life" and the two became fast friends, with Redmond teaching Chaplin sign language. Chaplin gave him space for an artist's studio on his movie lot and cast Redmond in seven of his films. Redmond was a member of the California Art Club, the San Francisco Art Association, the Laguna Beach Art Association and the Bohemian Club.

Ralph William Holmes (1876 – 1963) *Trees*
Oil on canvas Jonathan Club, #620

Holmes was born in La Grange, Illinois, and studied at Northwestern University, the Art Institute of Chicago and in Paris. He taught at the Carnegie Institute of Technology in Pittsburgh and at the Otis Art Institute in Los Angeles. He moved to Atascadero where he painted a number of murals. He painted landscapes of Yosemite, Bryce Canyon and the California desert and hills. This painting was purchased by the Club in 1984 when it renewed its interest in its art collection and began to make new purchases.

As the Club moved into its new Town Club building Mrs. Gertrude Matern, widow of the former Club manager, William A. Matern, donated a painting "Ducks in a Pond," by Dutch painter, Willi Teidjens. The painting is still part of the Club's collection.

In 1930, the second artist was elected to Artist Life Membership, George K. Brandriff, a dentist who had turned to painting full time two years earlier. Although mostly self-taught, he had studied with Jack Wilkinson Smith, member A-1. Two of Brandriff's paintings are still in the Club today: "Fisherman's Warf" and a work entitled "Tony's Wife."

John Stark Gorby was admitted as an Artist Life Member in 1931, but none of his paintings remain in the Club's art collection today. In 1931, Stanislaus Pociecha Poray, an artist born in Poland and imprisoned in Siberia following the Bolshevik revolution, was admitted as an Artist Member with the donation of a painting "Break, Break, Break" (no longer in the Club), and upgraded to the status of an Artist Life Member in 1948. One of his portraits, believed to be of early Jonathan Club member Charles L. Haskell, is still in the Club.

In July of 1932, in the deepening Depression, Dalzell H. Hatfield, a Resident Member, was transferred to Artist Life Membership, perhaps because of the art he brought to the club as a dealer, rather than as an artist.

A month later, the artist who would become the most significant of all of the Club's Artist Life Members was admitted as its sixth Life Artist member, Theodore Nikolai Lukits. The Club holds hundreds of this important artist's works because he and his wife, Lucille, donated over 360 of his pastels and oils to the Club in 1990.

Lukits was born in Hungary in 1897. He studied at Washington University and the Art Institute of Chicago, moving to Los Angeles in 1922. He became a successful portraitist and pastel artist. Around 1940, he started the Lukits Academy of Fine Arts, where he guided some of Southern California's most successful landscape and figurative artists. Lukits is known for his plein air landscapes, many painted at night with a miner's helmet-type hat. When he died in 1992 the Los Angeles Times called him "the last representative of California's plein-air painters." He was also the last living Artist Life Member of the Club.

As the Depression deepened, Charles Haskell (believed to be the subject of Stanislaus Poray's portrait) was given a room in the Club in exchange for looking after the Club's art collection.

Lewis E. Gumplo's dues were waived for life in 1947 because of art he had given the Club in an association that dated back to 1934. None of his paintings are currently in the Club.

In 1933, an Artist Membership was granted to Charles L. A. Smith, in exchange for one of his paintings. Smith's studio was a suite of rooms on the Twelfth Floor. In 1937, Smith was serving as the Club's "librarian and art connoisseur" overseeing the Club's books and having replaced Poray as the custodian of the art collection. Eight of Charles L. A. Smith's works are in the Club today, including a portrait of Charles Haskell, presented to the Club in 1935. Thus Charles Haskell is the subject of two portraits at the Club, by two of its Life Artists.

Another Artist Life Member was Arthur Beaumont, the celebrated naval artist and the painter of the mural for whom the Fourth Floor Cabrillo Room is named. Naval Reserve Commander Arthur Edwaine Beaumont was born in England in 1890. He opened an art studio in 1917, but fared so poorly that he pursued art studies in Los Angeles, London, Amsterdam and Paris. Returning to Southern California in 1926, he never again had trouble selling his art. He was an official artist for the U.S. Navy for over a half century, beginning in 1933 when he painted formal portraits of Naval officers, and one of these, Vice Admiral William D. Leahy, suggested that he paint studies of the U.S. Navy Fleet. Beaumont accepted a Naval Reserve commission as a lieutenant. The Los Angeles *Evening Herald and Express* called Beaumont "America's foremost military artist."

"Beau" helped raise funds for a heavy cruiser named for Los Angeles with a lithograph of the ship, prepared from blueprints, which was given to every purchaser of extra war bonds during the July, 1943, campaign. That image appeared in numerous ads and on posters and billboards, helping raise $80,371,372 and Beaumont personally raised $1.5 million for the campaign. The original sepia watercolor work from which that famous lithograph was taken was donated to the Jonathan Club in 1948 by John Urquhart Birnie along with two other Beaumont watercolors and an oil painting of the

Christian Siemer (1874 – 1940) *View Of Pasadena*
Oil on canvas, Jonathan Club, #658

Although not signed, this painting is almost certainly a work of Christian Siemer, the muralist who painted two of the other works hanging in the Florentine Lounge. This huge work, 10 x 17 feet, depicts Pasadena's Arroyo Seco in about 1932. The Rose Bowl is visible in the Arroyo to the left. The painting must have been commissioned for a very large space, perhaps for the Arroyo Vista Hotel which it features so prominently. It was discovered rolled up in storage in the Palm Springs area and purchased by the Club. Unfortunately, the Club then framed it…unfortunately, because the framed painting was then too large fit through the doors into the Club. A crane had to be hired to bring the painting into a third floor window. A photograph of the painting hangs today in the old Arroyo Vista Hotel, which today houses the Ninth Circuit Federal Court of Appeals.

Christian Siemer (1874 – 1940) *Huntington Library*
Oil on canvas, Jonathan Art Foundation #438

Siemer was born in New Zealand and came to Los Angeles in 1906. He was soon painting promotional mural-size paintings for the Chamber of Commerce for its campaign to attract new residents to the area. Siemer remained active in Southern California for the rest of his life. Three of Siemer's works hang in the Florentine Lounge. They are typical of his work in featuring architectural forms.

battleship USS *New Mexico*. Beaumont had begun his association with the Jonathan Club in 1947 with a different painting of USS *Los Angeles*, an artwork no longer in the Club. Two of Birnie's watercolor gifts are no longer in the Club.

By 1949, the Club had made Beaumont an Artist Life Member, conferring on him the number A-5, even though more than four such artists had preceded him. One of the Club's Life Artists had run up unpaid bills in a reciprocal club and had been stripped of his Life Artist status, and others may have fallen into disfavor as well.

The Club displays seven of Beaumont's works in the Town Club card room, including a 1952 watercolor of the frigate USS *James C. Owens*, a ship named for a Jonathan Club member who was killed in the Battle of Midway. The work was paid for by friends of the hero's father, James C. Owens, Sr.. The Beaumont works all celebrate ships of the U.S. Navy, which the artist described as "a protective and not aggressive force." In 1955, Beaumont was commissioned to paint a mural in the Town Club's Marine Room. He was paid $3,750, including the expenses of "a special canvas, paint, a helper, hanging and rental of costumes," and upon completion in 1956 the room was renamed for the subject of his grand mural, the "Cabrillo Room."

In 1948 and 1949, Beaumont produced 15 watercolors for covers of *The Jonathan* magazine, including a whimsical "Brother Jonathan Centennial Series" honoring the state's 100th birthday, a New Year's cover for 1949 and depictions of California missions. Copies of the Mission covers, "suitable for framing," were sold at the cigar stand. Beaumont died in 1978.

The Club abolished the Artist Life Member category in 1979. The Life Member concept, under which a member got certain privileges for life, was a thing of the Jonathan Club's past by then.

In 1985, the Club revitalized its art collection, sparked by its Art and Library Committee, headed by Paul Chevalier. Nancy Moure, former assistant curator of American Art at the Los Angeles County Museum of Art, was hired as the Club's art consultant. Moure was an authority on the art of early California. In 1987, the Jonathan Art Foundation was formed as a non-profit organization to purchase art to be displayed in the Jonathan Club and in schools and other non-profit institutions.

Today, about half of the art in the Jonathan Club belongs to the Jonathan Art Foundation and about half belongs to the Club itself. The total value is estimated at roughly $6 million, divided half and half between Club and Foundation.

In 1991, a Resident Artist category was added to the bylaws. This new category was a variation of the regular Resident Membership, with a few caveats. It served much the same purpose as the old Artist Life Membership but had slightly different rules. The Club currently has three Resident Artists, whose memberships are offset by contributions of their art, Robert Glenn Ketchum, Gerald Brommer and Dennis McNeil.

The first of the Resident Artists was the celebrated nature photographer Robert Glenn Ketchum, born in 1947. Ketchum's work has been featured in over 400 one-man shows worldwide since 1968. His photography and his books help him weigh in on national and international issues important to him, such as timber reform and Federal land management.

Gerald Brommer is an artist, author, educator and editor whose paintings are represented in over 4,100 private collections around the world and in the permanent collections of numerous corporations and educational institutions. He has authored more than 15 books and his art has been featured in more than 150 one-man shows and more than 200 group exhibitions. Most of his Jonathan Club art is found at the Beach facility.

The other is a first for the art program at the Jonathan Club, a performing rather than a visual artist, virtuoso tenor Dennis McNeil. McNeil has distinguished himself on the Broadway stage, the opera stage, in front of a symphony as a soloist, and singing Irish Folk Music. He has performed with the New York Metropolitan Opera, New York City Opera, San Francisco Opera, New Orleans Opera and Los Angeles Opera. Most importantly he now performs regularly for important events in the stately rooms of the Jonathan Club.

Jean Mannheim (1863-1945) *Blue Desert Foothills*
Oil on canvas, Jonathan Art Foundation #730

Mannheim, born in Germany, shifted from portraits to landscapes after he came to the United States. He was active in the influential Arroyo art colony of Pasadena and Highland Park which included architects such as the Greene brothers (Gamble House), writers and artists. The Jonathan Art Foundation purchased this painting of desert sand dunes and bare mountains in 1989.

Hanson Duvall Puthoff (1875 – 1972) *East Sierra Landscape*
Oil on lined canvas, Jonathan Art Foundation #384

Puthoff, an American, founded the L. A. Art Club. Two works of this famous artist hang in the Club. This work captures a scene along the east slope of the Sierra Nevada Mountains before the snow has fully melted. The Club engaged Puthoff to paint a portrait of its first president, George Alexander, in about 1905. During the 1920s Puthoff painted the animal dioramas in the Los Angeles Museum of Natural History.

Charles L.A. Smith (1871 – 1937) *Through The Sycamores*
Oil on canvas, Jonathan Club #662

Smith moved to Los Angeles in the 1920s and became a Life Artist Member of the Club in 1933, with the presentation of this painting. Smith served as the Club's "librarian and art connoisseur," overseeing the Club's books and art collections. This is one of eight of Charles L. A. Smith's works in the Club today.

Angel Espoy (1879 – 1963) *Monterey Dunes*
Oil on canvas, Jonathan Art Foundation #660

Espoy was born in Spain and sailed with the Spanish merchant marine. He moved to San Francisco in 1914 and to Los Angeles in 1922. While in the Bay Area he drew cartoons for movies. Espoy is known for his seascapes and maritime subjects.

Jack Wilkinson Smith (1873 -1949) *Mountain Glacier*
Oil on canvas, Jonathan Club #669

Smith was born in New Jersey, studied at the Art Institute of Chicago and the Cincinnati Art Academy and was a commercial artist in Lexington, Kentucky, and a staff artist with the *Cincinnati Enquirer*. He gained national fame for his sketches on the battle lines of the Spanish-American War. He settled in Southern California in 1906 and traveled the state painting its mountains, missions, coastal areas and canyons. He set up a home studio in "Artists Alley," a eucalyptus grove in Alhambra where Norman Rockwell was among his neighbors. Jack Wilkinson Smith was the first Jonathan Club Life Artist Member.

Ransom G. Holdredge (1836 – 1899) *Indian Encampment In The Sierras*
Oil on canvas, Jonathan Art Foundation #602

Holdredge was born in New York and came to San Francisco in 1858. He spent two years in France and returned to San Francisco where he earned local fame. He was thought by some critics of the time to be a better painter than his contemporary, William Keith. Holdredge was a co-founder of the San Francisco Art Association and was a member of the Bohemian Club. His paintings sold well, but the money flowed through his hands. His alcoholism seems to have compromised the quality of his paintings in later life. Holdredge was known for his painting of Indian subjects in the Sierras, but has been mostly forgotten since he died.

Maurice Braun (1877 – 1941) *Mountain Shadows*
Oil on lined canvas, Jonathan Art Foundation #656

Braun was an early California impressionist who was born in Hungary and came to New York with his family at the age of four. He left his apprenticeship to a jeweler to study at the National Academy of Design with William Merrit Chase. He painted portraits and figures in New York, spent a year in Europe, then came to San Diego in 1910 and stayed there. He painted the Southwest desert, the hills of Southern California and the High Sierras and was a devoted member of the Theosophical Movement.

Charles Reiffel (1862 – 1942) *Landscape*
Oil on canvas, Jonathan Art Foundation #866

Reiffel spent most of his life in New York, but moved to San Diego in 1925, painting the back country landscape of the area. He is considered to be one of the most important Southern California landscape impressionists.

Arthur Beaumont (1890 – 1978)
New Arrival, USS Los Angeles Joins the Fleet
Watercolor on paper, Jonathan Club #370

This was the first painting of the ship named for Los Angeles and Beaumont painted it from plans. From this study he produced an illustration that was copied thousands of times onto posters and billboards to help raise $8.5 million to pay for the cruiser's construction. It was presented to club by John Urquehart Birnie in 1948.

William Keith (1838 – 1911)
Mount Shast and Spirit Lake
Oil on lined canvas, Jonathan Club #650

Keith was born in Scotland and is one of the most famous of the late 19th-century California landscape artists. Known as the "Dean of California Artists" and "California's Old Master," he was a friend of Jonathan Club member John Muir. This 1879 painting was purchased by the Club in 1915 for $275 and today is probably the most valuable piece of art in the Club. It was placed on loan to a private school which did not value the painting and it was badly damaged by students who used it for target practice. The school paid a substantial sum for its restoration. It was returned to the Club in 1973.

Theodore Nikloai Lukits (1897 – 1992) *Grand Canyon*
Oil on lined canvas, Jonathan Art Foundation #661

Lukits was born in Hungary and came to Los Angeles in 1922. The last Artist Life Member of the Jonathan Club, Lukits and his wife, Lucille, donated over 360 of his works of art to the Jonathan Art Foundation. Lukits' pastels and watercolors, painted throughout the Southwest, were plein air studies for possible paintings. Lukits' works hang throughout the Jonathan Town Club and Beach Facility.

Theodore Lukits (1897-1992) *Spanish Senorita*
Pastel and gouache on paper, Jonathan Art Foundation

This is one of Lukits' works from the 1930s. Gouache is a technique of painting using opaque water-based paints. Lukits visited bars on Olvera Street and elsewhere in Los Angeles to paint Spanish and gypsy entertainers.

Henry Chapman Ford (1828-1894) *Santa Barbara Mission*
Oil on canvas, Jonathan Club #667

Henry Chapman Ford was born in Livonia, New York, and studied art in Paris and Florence before serving in the Civil War, where he drew illustrations for the press. After his discharge he moved to Chicago, then to Colorado and ultimately, in 1875, to Santa Barbara where he lived out his life. For 13 years he traveled by horse and buggy to California's 21 missions, producing etchings, watercolors and paintings that documented the missions' appearance in those years. His art was partially responsible for the missions' restoration.

Gerald Brommer (1927 -) *Palm Canyon*
Watercolor on paper, Jonathan Club #442

Brommer is a native of Los Angeles and a current Resident Artist member of the Club. His paintings can be found in over 4,100 private and institutional collections around the world. He is a prolific author and tireless leader of watercolor and collage workshops for artists around the world.

Jack Wilkinson Smith (1873 – 1949)
Marine Coastal Landscape
Oil on canvas, Jonathan Club #654

Four of his paintings hang in the Club today, including this one, painted in 1930 and donated to the Club by the artist.

Frank William Cuprien (1871-1948) *The Incoming Tide*
Oil on canvas, Jonathan Art Foundation #377

Cuprien was born in Brooklyn and studied art and music in New York, Philadelphia, Munich and Paris. Returning to the United States, he lived in Florida and Texas before moving to Southern California in 1912. Known for his seascapes and coastal scenes, he lived in Santa Monica and on Catalina Island before distinguished himself in the Laguna Beach art community. He was a founder and president of the Laguna Beach Art Association and a member of the California Art Club.

Robert Glenn Ketchum (1947-)
John Hopkins Inlet, Glacier Bay
Cibachrome photograph, Jonathan Art Foundation #439

Ketchum is a current Resident Artist, and is among the most important of today's landscape photographers. Ketchum took this photograph of Glacier Bay from his kayak in 1988 as part of his Tongass Project. Dozens of his photographs are in the Town Club and represent a number of his major projects over the years. He has published nine books of his work. Other books have been written about him.

George Kennedy Brandriff (1890 – 1936) *Fisherman's Wharf*
Oil on canvas, Jonathan Club, #785

Brandriff was born in Millville, New Jersey, graduated from the dental school of the University of Southern California (a dental school founded by Dr. Lewis E. Ford, a founding member of The Jonathan Club) and practiced dentistry in Hemet, California. Although mostly a self-taught weekend painter, he did study with a few local artists, including Jack Wilkinson Smith, the first of the Jonathan Club's Life Artists. Brandriff became the Club's second Life Artist in 1930. He enjoyed traveling with Hanson Puthuff, whose work is displayed in the Town Club Lobby along with one of the Club's two Brandriff paintings. He taught painting in Laguna Beach where he was president of the Laguna Beach Art Association. He painted many of his works around the Orange County coastline. He was diagnosed with cancer at a relatively young age and took his own life.

Millard Owen Sheets (1907 – 1989) *Fisherman's Wharf, San Francisco*
Watercolor on paper, Jonathan Art Foundation, #553

Sheets was born in Pomona, lived much of his life in Southern California and was a member of the Laguna Beach Art Association. He studied in Paris and at Chouinard Art School in Los Angeles and became director of the Otis Art Institute. He was a noted watercolorist, and also a painter, muralist, etcher, architectural designer and illustrator. He focused on landscapes and people in humble settings in mostly California settings. He is remembered for his murals and mosaics and for his designs on numerous Home Savings & Loan buildings.

THE SUM OF A GREAT CLUB

The vital statistics of the Jonathan Club (2005, unless otherwise noted):

Total Members: 3590
Resident Members: 2970
Junior Members: 400
Other categories of Members: 220
Emeritus Members (over 50 years in the Club): 35
Members living outside California: 183
Total employees during peak summer season: 682 during 2004
Average number of employees during the year: 420 in 2004
Average service length of employees: 6 years
Number of current employees with 25 plus years of service: 22
Reciprocal clubs: 59 (in 12 countries)
Books in the Library: 6,500
Bottles of wine: 25,000
Different wines: 1,100
Wines on Town Club wine list: 450
Value of wine in the Club: $2 million
Most expensive bottle of wine: $2,500
Meals served at the Town Club annually (2004): 159,676
Meals served at the Beach Facility annually (2004): 128,894
Number of Club events annually (2004): 180
Silverware: 13,875
Plates: 14,343
Glassware: 14,856
Daily copies of the Los Angeles Times*: 62*
Beach umbrellas: 308

The Jonathan Club is a private club organized exclusively for social, educational, recreational and fraternal purposes. The Jonathan Club members share similar social and educational backgrounds, and expectations of dress and behavior. Those joining the Club must be proposed by existing members and be vetted through a process that weighs carefully the prospect's compatibility with the existing membership. The Club long ago dropped any filter of ethnicity, gender, religion, national origin or sexual orientation, but rigorously preserves the social commonality that has brought its members meaning in the past and which guarantees that bond for the future. In short, men and women join the Jonathan Club to be with friends they've never met.

Even in the depths of a Depression that was dooming the Club, it stuck doggedly to its rigorous standards of admission, knowing that that was what most defined the Club and was most essential to its continued life.

That the Club flourishes over 100 years after its founding is a testament to the need it fills in Los Angeles. Its original members arrived at their clubhouse in horse-drawn carriages or the just-invented electric trolleys. The world around the Jonathan Club adjusted to the new technologies of the automobile, airplane, radio, cell phones and computer, but the polite camaraderie and shared culture within the walls of the club have remained constant. The attempted use of a cell phone in a public room of the Jonathan Club would cause as much amazement to the assembled members today as it would have in 1895. A Jonathan Club member of today, just as a counterpart in 1895, could easily converse about drama, music and the cultural and political events in the city. Members of every generation of Jonathans have adorned the walls of their clubhouse with distinguished art and a décor of understated elegance.

The changes in American culture over the last century have changed its club culture. Dots of concentrated cities diffused into blurs of suburbs and exurbs, and town clubs were augmented by country clubs. The ritual of after-work drinking fell to a custom of after-work fitness sessions, and this change diminished the importance of a town club tap room. As Robert Putnam's seminal book, *Bowling Alone*, so poignantly described, our society of cable television and Internet has turned us from a culture which gathered together to a landscape of isolationists.

And yet the Jonathan Club has never been stronger than it is today. Why? The Jonathan Club is almost unique among America's major social clubs in having two facilities, one downtown and the other at the beach. The Jonathan Beach Facility, so long viewed as an unjustifiable expense, is today a strong co-partner facility to the Town Club. The two entities satisfy different needs of the same urban leader. A typical pattern of Jonathan Club life over past decades has been for a younger member with a growing family to spend more time at the Beach Facility, and spend more and more time at the Town facility as an empty-nester. Today's Jonathan Club is Two Facilities/One Club. Its duality is one of its key strengths.

The Jonathan Club has been a special place for 110 years and is as special today as it has ever been. This is its story.

Appendices

References

Chapter 1 – Beginnings

The Original Jonathan Club – 1894
Los Angeles Express, April 30, 1894, p.8
Los Angeles Express, May 5, 1894, p.8
Los Angeles Express, April 27, 1894, p. 8
Los Angeles Times, May 8, 1894, p. 10
Los Angeles Herald, May 9, 1894
Los Angeles Times, October 19, 1894, p.10
Los Angeles Times, September 9, 1894, p. 7
Los Angeles Times, September 8, 1894, p. 3
Los Angeles Times, May 20, 1894, p. 10
Los Angeles Express, May 8, 1894
Los Angeles Times, July 28, 1894, p.4
Los Angeles Times, July 28, 1894, p.4
Los Angeles Times, August 5, 1894, p. 6
Roseman, Curtis C.; Wallach, Ruth; Taube, Dace; McCann, Linda; DeVerteuil, Geoffrey, The Historic Core of Los Angeles. Charleston: Arcadia Publishing, 2004

Was the Club founded to support William McKinley?

The Life of William McKinley. New York, P. F. Collier & Son, 1901
Fallows, Samuel, Life of William McKinley – Our Martyred President, Chicago: Ragan Printing House, 1901
Los Angeles Times, August 21, 1913, p. II5
Los Angeles Herald, May 5, 1894, p. 10
Los Angeles Times, September 6, 1894, p.4
Los Angeles Times, September 8, 1894, p. 3

How did the Jonathan Club get its name?

Bushnell, John. Jonathan Club brochure, 1926 (Los Angeles Times, Sept. 24, 1927, p. A1)
Morgan, Winifred. An American Icon – Brother Jonathan and American Identity. Newark: University of Delaware Press, 1988
Nye, Russel. The Unembarrassed Muse, New York: The Dial Press, 1970

Brother Jonathan and Jonathan Trumbull

Morgan, Winifred. An American Icon – Brother Jonathan and American Identity. Newark: University of Delaware Press, 1988
Roth, David M., Connecticut's War Governor: Jonathan Trumbull
Los Angeles Times, May 29, 1898
Ketchum, Alton. Uncle Sam – The Man and the Legend. New York: Hill & Wang, 1959

A social club is chartered – 1895

Los Angeles Times, June 9, 1895, p. 10
The Jonathan Club brochure, 1896-7
Bushnell, John. Jonathan Club brochure, 1926
Young, Betty Lou. Our First Century – The Los Angeles Athletic Club 1880-1980. Los Angeles: LAAC Press, 1979, p.17
Clark, David L. A History of the California Club. Los Angeles: The California Club, 1997, p.3
Union League Club of Los Angeles of Los Angeles Twenty-Fifth Anniversary, Los Angeles: Harry T. Watson, 1914
The Jonathan magazine, October, 1950, p.7

George L. Alexander and Ferd K. Rule

Pitt, Leonard and Pitt, Dale. Los Angeles A to Z – An Encyclopedia of the City and County. Berkeley: University of California Press, 1977.
Los Angeles Times, October 17, 1898, p.5
San Francisco Chronicle, August 20, 1913, p. 1

Founding fathers of The Jonathan Club

Benjamin F. Day
  Los Angeles City Directory
  1895 photo of Spring Street
  Los Angeles Times, July 23, 1889, p.2
Bradner W. Lee
  Lummis, Charles F., "Los Angeles and Her Makers," Out West Magazine 6, Los Angeles, April, 1909
  Guinn, A History of California – Biographical – III, Los Angeles: Historical Record Co., 1915
  McGroarty, John Steven, From the Mountains to the Sea, Chicago: The American Historical Society 1921
  Los Angeles City Directory
George Taylor
  Los Angeles Times, February 17, 1921, p. II3
George C. Gaskill
  Los Angeles City Directory
Charles H. White
  Los Angeles City Directory
Ferdinand K. Rule
  Los Angeles Times, July 5, 1898, p. A20
  Los Angeles Examiner, April 16, 1908, p. 1
  Los Angeles Herald, April 17, 1908, p.1
  Los Angeles Times, April 16, 1908, p.16
  Los Angeles Times, September 25, 1908, p.9
  Men of California 1900-1902
George L. Alexander
  Los Angeles City Directory
  Hancock Banning
  Los Angeles City Directory
  Spaulding, William A., History of Los Angeles City and County – III, Los Angeles: J. R. Finnell and Sons Publishing Co., 1931
  McGroarty, John Steven, California of the South – A History, Vol. V. Chicago: S. J. Clarke Publishing Co., 1935
  Hancock Banning personal papers, Huntington Library
  Who's Who in California 1928-29. San Francisco: Who's Who Publishing Co., 1929
Edward B. Tufts
  Los Angeles City Directory
  Los Angeles Times, September 24, 1927, p. A1
  Smith, Will, The Golfer Magazine, Winter Issue 2003
  Southern California Golf Association web site, 2003

The move from 132 Spring Street (The Huntington Years)

Los Angeles Times, November 21, 1902
Fredricks, William B., Henry E. Huntington and the Creation of Southern California, Columbus: Ohio State University Press, 1992
Clark, p. 39
Los Angeles Times, November 21, 1902
Board minutes, May 14, 1906
Los Angeles Examiner, April 30, 1904, p. 8
Los Angeles Times, August 13, 1903, p. 7
Board minutes, March 31, 1905
Board minutes, February 22, 1923
Board minutes, June 17, 1904
Board minutes, October 27, 1904
Board minutes, January 13, 1905
Board minutes, January 17, 1905
Los Angeles Times, January 27, 1905
Board minutes, February 10, 1905
Los Angeles Times, August 20, 1906, p. I12
The Jonathan magazine, October, 1944, p. 23
Board minutes, June 9, 1905
Board minutes, August 12, 1905
Board minutes. April 5, 1915
Board minutes, May 17, 1915
Los Angeles Times, July 5, 1898, p. A20
Los Angeles Examiner, April 16, 1908, p. 1
Los Angeles Herald, April 17, 1908, p.1
Los Angeles Times, April 16, 1908, p.16
Los Angeles Times, September 25
Board minutes, May 8, 1908
Art at the Jonathan Club, Jonathan Art Foundation

The strange club that moved into The Jonathan Club's old quarters

The Jonathan Club Board minutes, Jan 13, 1905
The Jonathan Club Board minutes, Jan 17, 1905
Los Angeles Times, September 24, 1904, p. A1
Los Angeles Times, October 2, 1904, p. 6
Los Angeles Times, November 19, 1904, p. 12
Los Angeles Times, November 29, 1904, p. A1
Los Angeles Times, January 20, 1905, p. I12
Los Angeles Times, February 1, 1905, p. I12
Los Angeles Times, March 21, 1906, p. I2
Los Angeles Times, March 23, 1906, p. II4
Los Angeles Times, March 22, 1906, p. II1
Los Angeles Times, March 26, 1906, p. II3
Los Angeles Times, July 27, 1906, p. II6

Pacific Electric Building

Leslie's Weekly, December 29, 1904, p. 628
Los Angeles Examiner, Sept 18, 1904, p. III-1
Fredericks, p. 60
Los Angeles Times, March 26, 1905, p. II1
Los Angeles Times, June 13, 1905, p.7

Henry Edwards Huntington

Fredericks Thorpe, James Ernest, Henry Edwards Huntington: A Biography. Berkeley: University of California Press, 1994.
Spurgeon, Selena A., Henry Edwards Huntington, his life and his collections. San Marino: Huntington Library, 1992
Clark, p. 45
Henry E. Huntington pamphlet, Huntington Library, undated
Los Angeles Examiner, Sep 18, 1904, p. III-1
Board minutes, March 31, 1905
The Jonathan magazine, May 1961

The avocado industry of Southern California began at the Jonathan Club

1936 Yearbook of the California Avocado Association
Shepherd, John and Bender, Gary, "A History of the Avocado Industry in California," California Avocado Society 2001 Yearbook 85: 29-50

The day police raided the California Club

Los Angeles Times, September 23, 1908, p. II 2
Los Angeles Examiner, September 23, 1908, p.1
Los Angeles Herald, September 23, 1908, p. 1
Board minutes, September 23, 1908
Los Angeles Times, November 16, 1909, p. II 1

The Jonathan Club of Mexico

Board Minutes, February 16, 1922
Board minutes, May 8, 1922
Special Membership Meeting minutes, May 23, 1922
Board minutes, September 26, 1922
Board minutes, December 23, 1925

UCLA was started at the Jonathan Club

Greenwald, Dave, "He Dreamed a Great University." UCLA Web Site, 2001

Other Facilities Considered by the Jonathan Club

Board minutes, May, 1912
Board minutes, December 12, 1913
Board minutes, May 29, 1914
Board minutes, October 20, 1921
Board minutes, February 16, 1922
Board minutes, June 1, 1922
Board minutes, October 3, 1922
Board minutes, April 21, 1927

Chapter 3 – Sixth and Figueroa

A home of its own

Board minutes, May 27, 1920
Los Angeles Examiner, Dec. 16, 1925
Board minutes, November 9, 1922
Board minutes, April 5, 1923
Board minutes, February 22, 1923
Board minutes, May 17, 1923
Club brochure, 1926
Board minutes, May 29, 1923

Board minutes, June 28, 1923
Board minutes, July 19, 1923
Board minutes, August 30, 1923
Board minutes, October 3, 1923
Board minutes, November 7, 1923
Board minutes, February 14, 1924
Board minutes, May 8, 1924
Board minutes, February 14, 1924
Board minutes, August 21, 1924
Board minutes, May 27, 1924
Board minutes, June 17, 1924
Board minutes, August 4, 1924
Board minutes, April 9, 1925
Board minutes, January 22, 1925
Board minutes, September 4, 1924
Board minutes, February 26, 1925
Los Angeles Times, April 17, 1925, p. 14
Map of Los Angeles, California. 1890, New York: Sanborn-Perris Map Co.

The Bellevue Terrace Hotel was here first

Dickenson, Brent C. A Visit to Old Los Angeles -- 14. Figueroa Street, California State University, Long Beach web site, 2003.
Massie, George, "Santa Clarita Valley History in Pictures – Newhall of the 1880s." Gold Prospector magazine, September 1989. Gold Prospectors Association of America.
Board minutes, December 13, 1923

A prestigious address: Grasshopper Street

comicsaccess.com, 2004
Map of Los Angeles, California. 1890, New York: Sanborn-Perris Map Co.
Kimball, Bernice, Street Names of Los Angeles
Los Angeles: City of Los Angeles Bureau of Engineering, 1988

Sixth and Figueroa becomes home

Clark, p. 68
Los Angeles Examiner, December 16, 1925
Gebhard, David and Winter, Robert, Los Angeles – An Architectural Guide. Gibbs-Smith Publisher. Salt Lake City. 1994
Los Angeles Times, July 22, 2004, p. B2
Jonathan Club brochure, 1926
"The Club With a Garage." Jonathan Club brochure circa 1925
Board minutes, October 1, 1925
Board minutes, March 4, 1926
Pitt Board minutes, October 15, 1925

William Parrish Jeffries: President in the best of times and worst of times

Who's Who in California – 1928-29. San Francisco: Who's Who Publishing Co., 1929
Jonathan Club Roster 1905
Board minutes, May 14, 1923
Board minutes, July 23, 1923
Jonathan Club brochure, 1926
Board minutes, August 27, 1930
Board minutes, September 12, 1930

Suppliers to The Jonathan Club 1925
Board minutes, July 24, 1924
The Architectural Digest, 1926

Schultze and Weaver – Premier architects for a premier club

Davis, Margaret L. The Los Angeles Biltmore: The Host on the Coast, p. 28
New York Times, August 26, 1951, p. 76
New York Times January 2, 1939, p. 26
Architectural Forum, September 1951, p. 68

Giovanni Battista Smeraldi -- The artisan who made the Town Club special

Davis Wolfe, W. C., Managing Editor, Men of California 1925-26

"Restoration Renders the Athenaeum Dusted Off, Shined Up, and More Authentic," Caltech News, California Institute of Technology. pr.caltech.edu 2003
Dawdy, Doris Ostrander, Artists of the American West, Vol. III, Athens, Ohio: Swallow Press/Ohio University Press, 1985
Falk, Peter Hastings, Who Was Who in American Art, Madison, Connecticut, 1985.
Goodstein, Judith R., "A Brief Commentary on the Athenaeum." Presentation to Caltech Associates, 1983.
New York Times, May 15, 1947, p. 26

Chapter 4 – Town Club Spaces

The Lobby: A grand entrance

Blueprints
Los Angeles Examiner, December 16, 1925
The Jonathan magazine, October, 1937, p.28
Board minutes, August 25, 1949
Board minutes, October 27, 1958
The Jonathan magazine, July 1970
The Jonathan, March, 1981, p.7

The Library: The Town Club's Inviolate sanctuary

Board minutes, October 13, 1905
Board minutes, February 26, 1906
Board minutes, February 27, 1906
Board minutes, June 4, 1934
Board minutes, October 25, 1966
Board minutes, December 8, 1905
The Jonathan magazine, October, 1934
The Jonathan magazine, January, 1938, p. 6

From Billiard Room to Tap Room

The Architectural Digest, 1926
The Jonathan magazine, June, 1942
The Jonathan magazine, January, 1955
The Jonathan magazine, October, 1954
Jonathan Club brochure, late 1950s

From Game Room to Grill Room

Architecture, October 1928
The Jonathan, May, 1961, p.7
The Jonathan magazine, February, 1947, p. 10
The Jonathan magazine, November 15, 1931, p.1
"Emergency" Supplement to The Jonathan, Nov, 1950?
Board minutes, March 29, 1983
Board minutes, April 26, 1983
Board minutes, December 12, 1916
The Jonathan magazine, April, 1947
The Jonathan magazine, May, 1947
The Jonathan magazine, March, 1937
The Jonathan magazine, September, 1939)
The Jonathan magazine, June, 1940
The Jonathan magazine, October, 1941, p. 5
The Jonathan magazine, July 1956
The Jonathan magazine, June, 1941, p. 16
The Jonathan magazine, November, 1936
The Jonathan magazine, March, 1993, p. 2
The Jonathan magazine, November, 1993, p.1
Board minutes, December 12, 1916

Reagan Room: From a women's refuge to a shrine for great Americans

Jonathan Club booklet, 1925
The Jonathan magazine, October, 1947
The Jonathan magazine, October, 1934
The Jonathan magazine, November, 1955
The Jonathan magazine, December, 1974
The Jonathan magazine, April, 1978
"House Tour Paper," January 15, 1988
The Jonathan magazine, July, 1996
The Jonathan magazine, January, 2001, p 2

The Florentine Lounge

Jonathan Club booklet, 1925
The Jonathan magazine, November 1, 1931, p. 2

The Jonathan magazine, August, 1971
The Jonathan magazine, November, 1973, p. 15

The Main Dining Room: The Club's gathering site

Jonathan Club booklet, 1925
The Jonathan magazine, October, 1941, p. 5

The Fourth Floor: A quiet setting for small meetings

The Jonathan magazine, February 2, 1943, p.9
Board minutes, March 24, 1955
Board minutes, October 1, 1956
The Jonathan magazine October, 1937, p. 38
The Jonathan magazine, October 10, 1975, p. 29
Board minutes, October 29, 1974
The Jonathan Magazine, March, 1955
The Jonathan magazine, October, 1983
The Jonathan, magazine, June, 1984
The Jonathan magazine, September, 1940

Sports and Fitness: The Club's midsection

Los Angeles Evening Examiner, Dec 16, 1925
The Jonathan magazine, April, 1953
Jonathan Club booklet, 1925
The Jonathan magazine, October, 1946
The Jonathan magazine, June, 1945
The Jonathan magazine, August, 1939
The Jonathan magazine, June, 1934
The Jonathan magazine, August, 1947
The Jonathan magazine, October 1, 1931
The Jonathan magazine, November, 1941
The Jonathan magazine, February, 1942
Board minutes, October 28, 1975
Board minutes, November 25, 1975
The Jonathan magazine, December, 1934
The Jonathan magazine, August, 1941
The Jonathan magazine, June, 1942
The Jonathan magazine, May, 1966
The Jonathan magazine, March, 1966
The Jonathan magazine, September, 1986
The Jonathan magazine, January, 1987
The Jonathan magazine, April 15, 1931
The Jonathan magazine, April, 1978

Residential Rooms: Important to the Town Club from the beginning

Board minutes, June 1, 1915
Board minutes, September 6, 1923
Board minutes, June 25, 1932
Board minutes, June 4, 1934

Sixth Floor

Board minutes, September 22, 1958
The Jonathan magazine, December, 1945
The Jonathan magazine, August, 1959

Seventh Floor

The Jonathan magazine, March, 1964
The Jonathan magazine, November, 1971
The Jonathan magazine, May, 1942

Eleventh Floor

Executive Committee minutes, August 17, 1951
The Jonathan magazine, March, 1941

Key Men: A legacy of Club dwellers

Web site usc.edu, Downtown Los Angeles Walking Tour, 2003
The Jonathan magazine, February, 1938, p. 11
The Jonathan magazine, October, 1937, p.23
The Jonathan magazine, June, 1987
The Jonathan magazine, January, 1940, p. 3
Board minutes, December 6, 1933

Thirteenth Floor: The floor that doesn't fit

Jonathan Club roster, 1924
Los Angeles Daily News, Aug 30, 1998, p. 13

Blueprints
L.A. Evening Examiner 12-16-25
The Jonathan Club magazine, July 1947
The Jonathan Club magazine, November, 1965
The Jonathan Club magazine, October, 1936
Jonathan Club brochure, c. late 1950s
The Jonathan Club magazine, March, 1965
The Jonathan Club magazine, June, 1941
The Jonathan Club magazine, December, 1943
The Jonathan Club magazine, November, 1944
The Jonathan Club magazine, June, 1940
The Jonathan Club magazine, November, 1960
Board minutes, February 25, 1964
The Jonathan Club magazine, May, 1941
The Jonathan Club magazine, July, 1968
Board minutes, January 24, 1961

Was there gambling in the Club?

Board minutes, July 13, 1932
Board minutes, November 30, 1932
Los Angeles Times, September 9, 1942, p. A3
Los Angeles Times, December 19, 1942
Board minutes, October 2, 1947
Board minutes, August 1, 1950

Chapter 5 – Depression

The Depression brings the Club to its knees

Board minutes, December 10, 1929
Board minutes, January 7, 1930
The Jonathan magazine, March 15, 1931
Board minutes, April 24, 1930
Board minutes, May 12, 1930
Board minutes, June 11, 1930
Board minutes, July 16, 1930
Board minutes, July 29, 1930
"Report of Committee of Seven Selected by Members of The Jonathan Club at Members Meeting, Monday, August 11, 1930," Aug18, 1930
Board minutes, September 10, 1930
Board minutes, September 30, 1930
Board minutes, September 11, 1930
Board minutes, November 26, 1930
Board minutes, April 15, 1931
Board minutes, July 8, 1931
Board minutes, October 8, 1930
Board minutes, January 6, 1932
Board minutes, February 3, 1932
Board minutes, October 29, 1930
Board minutes, August 19, 1931
Board minutes, August 31, 1931
Board minutes, October 7, 1931
Board minutes, December 31, 1931
Board minutes, August 31, 1932
Board minutes, October 5, 1932
Board minutes, September 22, 1933
Board minutes, May 24, 1933
Board minutes, April 14, 1933
Board minutes, March 31, 1933
Board minutes, June 28, 1933
Board minutes, July 12, 1933
Board minutes, July 26, 1933
Board minutes, August 11, 1933
Board minutes, September 6, 1933
Board minutes, September 22, 1933
Board minutes, May 21, 1930
Board minutes, May 12, 1930
Board minutes, May 6, 1930
Board minutes, July 29, 1930
Board minutes, September 3, 1930

The end and the Beginning: Sold on the Courthouse steps

Board minutes, May 8, 1933
The Jonathan magazine, August, 1965
Board minutes, June 7, 1933
(Board minutes, September 11, 1934
Letter from Warren E. Libby, Attorney, to Directors of Jonathan Club, January 25, 1941, included in Board minutes, January 31, 1941
Letter to members from Board, Mar 30, 1935
Los Angeles Times, April 11, 1935, p. A5
Board Minutes, Jonathan Club, 1935

Chapter 6 – Jonathan Club at the Beach

Life on the Beach

Board minutes, April 21, 1927
Los Angeles Times, November 29, 1964
Board minutes, March 28, 1934
The Jonathan magazine, July, 1935
Marquez, Ernest, Santa Monica Beach. Santa Monica: Angel City Press. 2004, p. 175
Board minutes, November 8, 1933
Los Angeles Times, June 27, 1926, p.E5
Board minutes, Mary 27, 1955
Board minutes, November, 1956
The Jonathan magazine, November, 1960, pp. 5-6
Board minutes, April 21, 1955
The Jonathan Magazine, August, 1944
The Jonathan magazine, June, 1943, p.6
The Jonathan magazine, July, 1944, p.13
The Jonathan magazine, June, 1947, p. 6
The Jonathan magazine, March, 1956
The Jonathan magazine, June, 1957, p. 4
Board minutes, September 26, 1967
The Jonathan magazine, June, 1957, p. 5
The Jonathan magazine, June, 1958
Board minutes, May 11, 1959
Board minutes, June 26, 1962
Board minutes, March 24, 1958
Board minutes, November 28, 1962
Board minutes, August 24, 1971
Board minutes, June 27, 1972
Santa Monica Outlook 4/9/65?
Board minutes, August 18, 1966
Board minutes, March 29, 1967
Board minutes, July 25, 1967
Board minutes, April 23, 1968
Beach Committee minutes May 8, 1968, included in Board minutes, May 27, 1968)
Board minutes, August 27, 1968
Board minutes, September 24, 1968
Board minutes, November 25, 1969
Board minutes, February 27, 1969
Board minutes, October 29, 1974
Board minutes, August 30, 1983
Board minutes, June 24, 1986
The Jonathan magazine, August, 1996, p. 4

Edgewater Club

Edgewater Club booklet, 1925
Los Angeles Times, August 30, 1925
Los Angeles Times, June 23, 1929, p. D8

The life cycle of the Edgewater Club

Los Angeles Times, June 23, 1929, p. D8
Los Angeles Times, September 10, 1948, p.7
Los Angeles Times, November 13, 1948, p. A7
Los Angeles Times, July 12, 1964, p. WS1
Los Angeles Times, November 29, 1964, p. WS3

Sea Breeze Beach Club and Beverly Beach Club

Los Angeles Times, June 20, 1926, p. F1
Los Angeles Times, June 17, 1926, p. 10
Los Angeles Times, June 27, 1926, p. E5
Letterhead of Sea Breeze Beach Club
Los Angeles Times, June 1, 1933, p. A2
Los Angeles Times, August 15, 1926, p. E7

Chapter 7 – War

If it's not a Depression it's a War! – The Club rebounds in the 1940s

Board minutes, April 9, 1941
Board minutes, July 25, 1941
Board minutes, December 5, 1944
Board minutes, December 23, 1941
Board minutes, February 3, 1942
Jonathan Club Army Navy Yearbook 1944-1945
The Jonathan magazine, June, 1944, p. 12
The Jonathan magazine, March, 1943
Board minutes, June 16, 1942
Board minutes, February 25, 1943
Board minutes, April 15, 1943
Board minutes, January 7, 1944
Board minutes, February 28, 1944
Board minutes, July 20, 1944
Board minutes, November 24, 1943
The Jonathan magazine, May, 1942
The Jonathan magazine, June, 1942, p. 17
Board minutes, September 24, 1945
Board minutes, December 4, 1945
Board minutes, January 7, 1946
Board minutes, October 1, 1946

Marion Flay Baugh Memorial Beacon

The Jonathan magazine, November, 1945
Board minutes, January 10, 1946
Marion Flay Baugh
    Ford, Daniel, Flying Tigers, Washington: Smithsonian Institution Press, 1991
    Bond, Charles R, Jr., and Anderson, Terry H., A Flying Tiger's Diary, College Station: Texas A & M University Press, 1984
    The Jonathan magazine, February, 1942
    The Jonathan magazine, April, 1942
John Thomas Dye
    State Summary of War Casualties from World War II for Navy, Marine Corps, and Coast Guard Personnel. Washington: U. S. Navy, 1946, p. 26
    The Jonathan magazine, September, 1945
    The Jonathan magazine, October 1945, p. 20
    Destroyer Escort Sailors Association web site, 2004
    Wikipedia, "USS Underhill (DE-682)"
Nathaniel G. Guiberson, Jr.
    History of the 307th Bomb Group/Wing, Website: http://5thbomberbarons.com/board/?topic=topic6, 2004
    The Jonathan magazine, August, 1941, p.8
    The Jonathan magazine, January, 1942, p.16
    Interview w/ Samuel Guiberson, Houston,TX, 2004
    Interview w/ Mrs. Jayne Copp Guiberson Berger, 2004
    Interview w/ Olga Poole, Frances C. Arrillaga Alumni Center, Stanford University
Abbott Q. Hastings
    State Summary of War Casualties from World War II for Navy, Marine Corps, and Coast Guard Personnel. Washington: U. S. Navy, 1946, p. 38
    National Personnel Records Center letter to Nat Read, October 21, 2004
    The Jonathan magazine, December, 1943
Fred J. Koebig
    Sakaida, Henry, The Siege of Rabaul. St. Paul: Phalanx Publishing Co., 1996
    State Summary of War Casualties from World War II for Navy, Marine Corps, and Coast Guard Personnel. Washington: U. S. Navy, 1946, p. 32
    Los Angeles Times, April 21, 1938, p A13
    Los Angeles Times, January 22, 1939, p. 11
    Los Angeles Times, April 21, 1939, p. A14
    Los Angeles Times, May 6, 1939, p. 3
    Los Angeles Times, May 10, 1939, p. A 18
    Los Angeles Times, May 13, 1939, p. 8
    Los Angeles Times, May 16, 1939, p. A
    Los Angeles Times, May 26, 1939, p. A3
    Los Angeles Times, October 4, 1939, p. 21
    Los Angeles Times, November 18, 1939, p. A7
    Los Angeles Times, December 13, 1939, p. A9
    Los Angeles Times, April 17, 1944, p. A8
    Los Angeles Times, May 22, 1944, p. A7
Roland McNaughton
    The Jonathan magazine, December, 1945, p. 26
James C. Owens, Jr.
    J. C. Owens DD776 Association
    The Jonathan magazine, September, 1942, p.15
Jack D. Roberts
    Los Angeles Times, August 3, 1944, p. 6
    Los Angeles Times, September 2, 1944, p. A1
    World War II Honor List of Dead and Missing Army and Army Air Forces Personnel from: California . Washington: U.S. War Department.
    National Archives and Records Administration letter to Captain Nat Read, November 19, 2004
    E-mail from Commander Jeff Loftus, Department of Homeland Security
    United States Coast Guard, Director, Motion Picture & Television Office, Los Angeles, November 4, 2004
    The Jonathan magazine, June, 1942, p.21

The Coast Guard at War: IV – Loran, Volume I, Washington: U.S. Coast Guard Office of Engineering, 1944, Section III, Chapter 4
Willoughby, Malcolm F., The U.S. Coast Guard in World War II. Annapolis, Md.: Naval Institute Press, 1957/1989

George Shirey
  The Jonathan magazine, July 1943, p. 11

Fred A. Steiner
  Ausland, John C., Letters Home: A War Memoir (Europe 1944-1945), Ch 2, "Keeping the Mem-ories Alive," website of John Davis, http://home .nc.rr.com/ww2memories/ww2.html, 2004
  Website of the National 4th Infantry (IVY) Division Association, http://www.4thinfantry.org/info.html
  The Jonathan magazine, October, 1943
  American Forces in Action, Utah Beach to Cherbourg (6 Jun – 27 June 1944), Washington: Historical Division, War Department, for the American Forces in Action series, 1948, p. 110

Harold O. Want
  The Jonathan magazine, October, 1943
  The Jonathan magazine, November, 1944
  The Jonathan magazine, August, 1945, p. 16

Louis Canepa sells the Jonathan Beach Club and loses his office

Board minutes, March 14, 1945
Board minutes, April 23, 1945
Board minutes, May 10, 1945
Board minutes, May 14, 1945
Board minutes, October 17, 1946
Board minutes, October 22, 1946
Board minutes, October 26, 1946
Board minutes, March 27, 1947
Board minutes, April 18, 1947

Chapter 8 – Recent Times

Postwar years: Much energy and potential mischief

Board minutes, May 27, 1955
Board minutes, June 27, 1955
Board minutes, September 22, 1958
The Wall Street Journal, December 24, 1958
Horn, Charles W., letter to the Club president, January, 1959, included in January 26, 1959 minutes of the Public Relations Committee and Board minutes of January 8, 1959
The Jonathan magazine, November, 1953
The Jonathan magazine, May 25, 1950
The Jonathan magazine, July, 1955
The Jonathan magazine, February, 1953
The Jonathan magazine, September, 1953
The Jonathan magazine, October, 1970
House Committee minutes, January 16, 1962, included in Board minutes, October 26, 1965
Board minutes, June 23, 1964
Board minutes, October 25, 1966
Board minutes, August 22, 1967
Board minutes, August 27, 1968
Board minutes, December 17, 1968
Board minutes, May 13, 1968
Board minutes, October 25, 1960
Board minutes, May 23, 1967
Board minutes, August 27, 1968
Board minutes, May 27, 1969
Board minutes, June 25, 1968
Board minutes, March 25, 1969
Board minutes, May 18, 1970
Board minutes, November 24, 1970
Board minutes, October 31, 1978
Board minutes, August 30, 1983
Board minutes, March 29, 1988
Board minutes, April 25, 1972
Board minutes, October 24, 1972
Board minutes, December 22, 1970
Board minutes, June 22, 1971
Board minutes, November 26, 1974
Board minutes, March 26, 1974
Board minutes, December 20, 1976

Los Angeles Times, June 27, 1989
Board minutes, August 24, 1971
Board minutes, March 27, 1973

A leaf is turned – into a model club

Los Angeles Times, July 26, 1985
Los Angeles Times, July 30, 1985
Los Angeles Times, October 12, 1988
Los Angeles Times, September 27, 1977
Board minutes, January 27, 1987
Los Angeles Times, April 30, 1987
Board minutes, April 28, 1987
Board minutes, April 28, 1987
Board minutes, May 26, 1987
Los Angeles Times, August 21, 1987
Clark, pp. 143-144
Board minutes, April 28, 1987
Los Angeles Times, January 7, 1988
Los Angeles Times, June 21, 1988

Chapter 9 – Art

Great clubs have great art

Board minutes, January 26, 1907
Board minutes, November 10, 1905
Board minutes, September 30, 1905
Board minutes, September 13, 1907
Board minutes, October 20, 1905
The Jonathan magazine, October, 1981, p.8
Board minutes, March 10, 1915
Board minutes, November 28, 1925
Board minutes, February 18, 1926
Board minutes, December 3, 1925
Board minutes, July 9, 1930
Board minutes, May 20, 1931
Board minutes, July 20, 1932
Los Angeles Times, February 8, 1992
The Jonathan magazine, March, 1987
Board minutes, June 7, 1933
Board minutes, June 27, 1934
Board minutes, February 26, 1947
Board minutes, August 11, 1933
The Jonathan magazine, March, 1937
Board minutes, January 16, 1935
Jonathan Art Foundation Notebook
Board minutes, December 17, 1953
Arthur Edwaine Beaumont – Naval Artist 1890-1978, the Beaumont Publishing Company. 1989
Board minutes, March 25, 1948
The Jonathan magazine, February, 1947
The Jonathan magazine, July, 1948
Board minutes, January 20, 1949
Board minutes, December 9, 1948
The Jonathan magazine, March, 1987
Board minutes, November 4, 1986
The Jonathan magazine, August, 1991

Index

A
Activities of the new club, 12
Air rights, 150
Alexander, George L.
    background, 19, 23
    death in 1913, 13
    portrait, 19
    president, 18
    room named after, 104
American Type Founders Company, 19
American with Disabilities Act, 133
Anders, William A., 97
Angeles Mesa Land Company, 45
Arcadia Hotel, 27
Arkell, W. J., 45
Art. See also Paintings
Artists' Life Membership, 154, 156, 158
    history, 154, 156, 158
    Jonathan Art Foundation, 158
Art Collections, 35
Artist Life Membership, 154, 156, 158
Atlantic Richfield Towers, 62, 147–148
Auditorium, Edgewater Club, 129
Austin, John, 35
Automobile. See Transportation
Avocado industry, 36
Axelrod, Bob, 138

B
Baker, Arthur E., 46
Banning, Carl Phineas, 121
Banning, Hancock, 23
Barber shop, 74, 76
Barker Brothers, 46
Bather's Cocktail Lounge, 130
Bather's Grill, 128
Baugh, Marion Flay, 138–139, 140–141
Beach Club
    Beverly Beach Club, 123, 134
    Depression impact, 121, 123
    Edgewater Club. See Edgewater Club
    financial difficulties, 126–127
    purchase, 53, 118–120
    sale of, 142–143, 148
    Sea Breeze Beach Club. See Sea Breeze Beach Club
    Westport Beach Club, 132
Beaumont, Arthur
    Artist Life Member, 158
    background, 156
    Cabrillo Landing painting, 104, 105
    military paintings, 156, 158
    New Arrival, USS Los Angeles Joins the Fleet painting, 163
    portrait of William D. Leahy, 156
    USS James C. Owens painting, 139, 158
    USS Los Angeles painting, 158
Beer steins, 85, 86, 89, 91
Bellevue Terrace Hotel, 48–49, 77
Belsey, George, 120
Beverly Beach Club, 123, 134
Big Pines facility, 39
Bilicke, A. C., 27
Billiard Room/Tap Room, 21, 33, 85–89
Biltmore Hotel, 56, 66, 114
Birnie, John Urquhart, 156, 158, 163
Biscailuz, Gene, 91
Bonfilio, Millie, 37
Bonfilio, N., 37
Borman, Frank, 97
Botanical Gardens, 35
Brandriff, George
    background, 167
    Fisherman's Wharf painting, 156, 167
    Tony's Wife painting, 156
Braun, Maurice, Mountain Shadows painting, 162
Breakfast Club, 103, 104
Brink, Beno, 143
Brommer, Gerald
    background, 158, 165
    Palm Canyon painting, 165
Brother Jonathan
    background, 14–15
    drawing, 17
    Jonathan Trumbull and, 17
Brown, Logan, 71, 96, 98
Buffet carriage, 91
Buildings
    Corfu Building. See Corfu Building
    Jonathan Club Building Company, Ltd., 46, 122
    original home, 10–11
    other facilities considered, 39
    Pacific Electric Building. See Pacific Electric Building
    Sixth and Figueroa. See Sixth and Figueroa location
    Town Club. See Town Club
Bull, John, 14
Bundy, C. L. and F. E., 134
Bundy, Thomas C., 134
Burgoyne, E. M., 23
Burkhart Investment Company, 45
Burnett, T. S., 123
Bushnell, John B.
    background, 23
    beginning of building construction, 46
    McKinley connection, 13
    naming of the Club, 18

C
California Avocado Association, 36
California Club
    discrimination, 151
    founding, 18
    hotel design, 56
    move to Hill and Fifth Streets, 26
    new building, 50
    police raid, 37
Calle de los Chapules, 49
Canepa, Louis, 127, 138, 142–143
Cannell & Chaffin, 71
Cape Cod Room, 114, 115
Card room, 33
Carlton Hotel purchase, 147
Carpenter, E. R., 118
Cartoons, 15, 93
Catalina Room, 133
Cattalucci's "The Combatants", 32, 154
Centennial, 150
Chamberlain, W. H., 18
Chandelier Room, 85–86
Charter, 18
Charters, George A., 38, 44–46
Chevalier, Paul, 158
Cigar counter, 70, 74
Cigar Society, 115
Clark, Rex. B., 120
Clawson, John Willard
    portrait of Ferd Rule, 19
    portrait of Henry E. Huntington, 34
Cleary, Warren, 19
Clemo, Bob, 19
Columbo, 15
Commercial Club, 27
Committee of Seven, 119–120
Common persons, 14
Condominiums, 150
Conversation Room, 30
Coogan, Nolan S., 123
Cooley, John B., 123
Copp, Andrew J., 138, 139
Corfu Building
    1896-1905 headquarters, 18, 27
    interior photos, 20, 21
    Occidental Club occupation, 27
Costumes, 41
Cronkite, Walter, 97
Cuprien, Frank William, Incoming Tide painting, 166
Cushman & Wakefield, 148

D
Dahlstrom, Ryno, 123
Day, Benjamin F., 22
De Baker Estate, 154
Del Mar Day, 147
Democrats, 1894 voters, 10
Denham, Chester, 113
Depression
    Club response, 121
    foreclosure of the Club, 122–123
    Grill Room buffet carriage, 91
    Grill Room rentals, 91
    impact on grand hotels, 57
    impact on the Club, 53, 118–121
    membership dues, 118, 121
    Town Club neglect, 71
Dewey, Admiral, 17
Dickson, Edward A., 39
Dillingham Corporation, 133, 148
Dining Room, 21, 33
Dirigo Club of San Francisco, 12
Discrimination, 149, 150–151
Dixon, Charles, 37
Dixon, Lawrence Murray, 56
Dole, Elizabeth Hanford, 97
Dress code, 127, 132, 149
Drug store, 51
Dufour, Joseph, 104
Dutton, Harry A., 51
Dwyer Studios construction documentation, 46
Dye, John Thomas, 141
Dylan, Bob, 149

E
Edgewater Club
    financial hardship, 126–127
    life cycle, 129
    operating hours during the War, 130
    physical attributes, 128–129
    purchase, 39, 118, 119
    renovations, 130, 132, 133
    sports and fitness, 128, 130, 132
Edwards, LeRoy M., 122, 129, 138
Eighth floor, 110, 112
Eisenhower, Dwight D., 139
Electric trolleys, 10
Elevators
    attendants, 75
    history, 75
    Ladies' elevator permanently closed, 148
    to Thirteenth Floor, 114, 115
    for women, 70, 75, 95–96, 148, 149
Eleventh floor, 110, 112
Employees, 30
English Automobile Club, 50
Entrance date discrepancy, 12
Erdman, Frank, 115
Espoy, Angel, Monterey Dunes painting, 160

F
Facilities considered by the Club, 39
Fife, Ralph E., 62
Fifth floor, 106–109
Figueroa Street, 49. See also Sixth and Figueroa location
Figueroa y Parra, José Secundino, 49
Finch, R. A., 76
Fine Craftsman Award, 62
Firefighting techniques, 10
First Mortgage Bonds, 122–123
First-aid room, 147
Fiske, Vern, 95
Fitzgerald, Louise M., 151
Fitzhugh, Thornton, 26, 28
Floral shop, 51
Florentine Lounge, 98
Ford, Gerald R. and Betty, 97
Ford, Henry Chapman, Santa Barbara Mission painting, 164
Founding
    background history, 10–11
    fathers, 22–23
    McKinley, William, support, 13
    political group, 12
    social group, 12–14, 18
    timeline, 10–11
Fourth floor, 104–105
Foyer, 20
French Pink Tennessee marble, 70, 71
Front entrance, 65
Fulton, Belle, 45

G
Gambling, 114–115
Game emporium, 51
Game locker for wild game, 103
Game Room, conversion to Grill Room, 90–93
Garage, 79, 147, 149
Gargoyles, 89, 93
Gartner, Lloyd P., 150
Gaskill, George C., 23
Gibson, Dunn & Crutcher law firm, 122
Gibson, Trask, Dunn & Crutcher, 37
Gideon Bibles, 112
Gift shop, 48, 77
Gladding, McBean & Co., 85, 89
Godfrey, Fritz, 115
Golden System Scalp Treatment, 76
Gorby, John Stark, 156
Gouache, 164
Graham, Billy, 97

Grand Central Terminal, 56
Grasshopper Street, 49
Grill Room
　booths and cubicles, 93
　conversion from Game Room, 90–93
　pictured, 67
Guerin, Arthur, 115
Guiberson, Nathaniel G., Jr., 141
Gumplo, Lewis E., 156
Gymnasium, 33

H
Hahn, Jim, 151
Haines Hall, 39
Harbor Parkway (Freeway), 60–61, 147
Haskell, Charles L., 156
Hastings, Abbott O., 141
Hatfield, Dalzell H., 156
Hearst, William Randolph, 129
Heinsbergen, A. T., 66, 71
Heinsbergen, Tony, 71
Heitschmidt, Earl T., 62, 79, 132
Heitschmidt, Jonathan Earl, 85
Hertrich, William, 36
Hightower, Dennis F., 151
Hi-Jinks stag party, 41, 115
History of the Jews of Los Angeles, 150
Holcomb Valley, 39, 126
Holdredge, Ransom G., Indian Encampment In The Sierras painting, 161
Hollenbeck Hotel, 12
Holmes, Ralph William, Trees painting, 155
Hope, Bob, 97
Horn, Charles W., 147
Horse race gambling, 115
Hosa Design Associates, 96
Houghton, Roy, 86
Huntington, Collis P., 35
Huntington, Henry Edwards
　Art Collections, 35
　Art Committee, 154
　avocado industry, 36
　background, 26, 34–35
　bar closing, 37
　Botanical Gardens, 35
Huntington Building, 32
Huntington Gardens, 36
The Huntington Library, 35, 157
　less Club involvement, 44
　library purchase, 81
　portrait, 34
　president, 19, 26, 35
　presidential legacy, 52
　room named after, 104
　Vice President, 19

I
Italian Renaissance
　1955 property sales, 146
　1970 renovation, 71, 149
　current décor, 79
　design of new home, 50
　Grill Room renovations, 93
　Main Dining Room, 103
　Sea Breeze Beach Club, 134

J
Jackson, Helen Hunt, "Ramona" novel, 48
"Jazz on the Roof", 115
Jeffries, Thomas L., 53
Jeffries, William Parrish
　background, 52–53
　cementing the cornerstone, 44
　Edgewater Club purchase, 126
　Jonathan Beach Club, 118–120
　portrait, 52
　resignation, 120
　room named after, 104
　Sixth and Figueroa location, 44–46, 52–53, 55
Jeffries, William T., 53
Johnson, Squire, 142–143
Jonathan. See Brother Jonathan
The Jonathan magazine
　bathing suit standards, 127
　Beach Club amenities, 127
　Beaumont covers, 158
　garage addition convenience, 147
　Grill Room sound-proofing, 93
　Jews as members, 150
　property sale notices, 130
　reorganization, 123
Jonathan Beach Club Co, Ltd. See Beach Club
Jonathan Club Band, 46
Jonathan Club Building Company, Ltd., 46, 122
Jonathan Club Glee Club, 46
Jonathan Country Club, 39
Jump, Gordon, 120
Jump, James. W., 44, 118

K
Keith, William
　background, 163
　Mount Shasta and Spirit Lake painting, 154, 163
Kennedy, John F., 13
Keogh Bros., 62
Ketchum, Robert Glenn
　background, 158, 166
　John Hopkins Inlet, Glacier Bay painting, 166
Key Men organization, 113
Kinsey Hall, 39
Knapp, Brooke, 151
Koebig, Fred J., 141
Kudrave, Peter, 71

L
La Fiesta de Los Angeles, 19
Ladies. See Women
Lange & Bergstrom, 46
Lauman, Jane, 70
Leahy, William D., 156
Lee, Bradner W., 23
Leslie's Weekly, 33
Library, 81–83
Lincoln, Abraham, 10, 15
Liquor
　private club licenses, 37
　Prohibition. See Prohibition
Lobby, Town Club
　ceilings, 67
　cigar counter, 70, 74
　description, 32, 70–71
　mezzanine, 70, 71, 73, 74
　pictured, 29
　renovations, 71–74
Lo-Jinks stag party, 41
Los Angeles Athletic Club, 18
"The Los Angeles Biltmore", 56
Los Angeles Club, 14, 18
Los Angeles Evening Herald and Express, Beaumont article, 156
Los Angeles Evening Herald, athletic club amenities, 51
Los Angeles Examiner
　California Club police raid, 37
　club garage, 79
　gymnasium, 33
　residential rooms, 33
　showpiece quarters, 32
　women's reception room review, 33
Los Angeles Express
　description of the new club, 12
　political editor Edward Dickson, 39
Los Angeles Herald
　opinion of the new club, 12
　residential rooms, 33
Los Angeles Herald-Express, copies available for patrons, 91
Los Angeles Republican Club, 12
Los Angeles Times
　Bonfilio article, 37
　construction accident, 46
　death of George Alexander, 13
　financial aid from owner, 18
　membership advertisement, 134
　residential rooms, 33
　Sea Breeze Beach Club article, 134
　slot machine removal, 115
Lounge, 98
Lovell, James A., Jr., 97
Lukits, Lucille, 156
Lukits, Theodore Nikolai
　background, 156, 163
　Grand Canyon painting, 163
　Spanish Senorita painting, 164
Lusitania, 27

M
Main Ballroom (Amusement Room), 28, 33
Main Dining Room
　background, 103
　Edgewater Club, 129
　pictured, 21, 67
Main Lounge, 98
Malone, Joseph J., 143
Mannheim, Jean, Blue Desert Foothills painting, 159
Margaret L. Davis, 56
Marine Room, 104
Marion Flay Baugh Memorial Beacon, 140–141
Markham, Henry, 12
Marshall, George C., 139
Martin, Albert C., 148
Masqueray, E. L., 56
Matern, William A. and Gertrude, 156
McDowell, E. E., 93
McKinley, William, 13
McNaughton, Roland, 141
McNeil, Dennis, 158
Media relations, 12
Memberships
　Artists' Life Membership, 154, 156, 158
　to cover Jonathan Club of Mexico expenses, 38
　Depression resignations, 121
　discrimination, 150–151
　dues during the Depression, 118–121
　Edgewater Club, 129
　honorary, 139
　Occidental Club, 27
　old and new Clubs, 123
　Regular Life Member, 118, 120
　Special Life Member, 118, 120
　transferable dues, 120
　for women, 150, 151
Metropolitan Club, 35
Mexican Jonathan Club, 38–39
Minamide, Daniel, 93
Monroe, Charles, 37
Moore, Ernest C., 39
Morgan, Lloyd, imaginary city painting, 56–57
Mountain Home facility, 39
Moure, Nancy, 158
Mural Dining Room, 129

N
Naming The Jonathan Club, 14–15
Napoleon statue, 154
Nerdrum, Jarl, 149
New England room, 104
New Orleans room, 104
Nicoll the Tailor, 18
Nimitz, Chester, 139
Ninth floor, 110, 112
Northridge Earthquake, 130
Nye, Russell, The Unembarrassed Muse, 14

O
Occidental Club, 26, 27
Ordayne, Neale, 52
Otis, Harrison Gray, 18
Owens, James C., Jr., 141
Owens, James C., Sr., 158
Oyster Bar, 115

P
P. J. Walker Co., 79
Pacific Electric Building
　ballroom, 28, 33
　billiard room/card room, 21, 33
　card room, 33
　Conversation Room, 30
　dining room. See Main Dining Room
　gymnasium, 33
　Jonathan Club's new headquarters, 26–27
　Lobby. See Lobby, Town Club
　Main Ballroom (Amusement Room), 28, 33
　physical attributes, 32–33
　Reading Room, 20, 29, 33, 81
　residential neighborhood, 33
　residential rooms. See Residential rooms
　roof garden, 29, 33, 115
　stage, 31
　stories, 36–39
　Tap Room, 21, 31, 85–89
　train station, 32, 33
　Turkish room, 33
Pacific Electric Company, 34–35
Pacific Electric Railway, 35, 44–45
Pacific Light and Power, 34
Pacific Mutual Life Insurance Company, 122–123
Pacific Room, 133
Paging system, 75

Paintings. See also Portraits
  Blue Desert Foothills, 159
  Break, Break, Break, 156
  Cabrillo Landing, 104, 105
  California Landscape, 154, 155
  Ducks in a Pond, 156
  East Sierra Landscape, 159
  Fisherman's Wharf, 156, 167
  Fisherman's Wharf, San Francisco, 167
  Grand Canyon, 163
  Huntington Library, 157
  imaginary city, 57
  Incoming Tide, 166
  Indian Encampment In The Sierras, 161
  John Hopkins Inlet, Glacier Bay, 166
  Landscape, 162
  Marine Coastal Landscape, 166
  Marine Oil Painting, 154
  Monterey Dunes, 160
  Mount Shasta and Spirit Lake, 154, 163
  Mountain Glacier, 161
  Mountain Shadows, 162
  New Arrival, USS Los Angeles Joins the Fleet, 163
  Palm Canyon, 165
  Santa Barbara Mission, 164
  Spanish Senorita, 164
  Through The Sycamores, 160
  Tony's Wife, 156
  Trees, 155
  USS James C. Owens, 139, 158
  USS Los Angeles, 158
  View of Pasadena, 157
Palisades Lounge, 133
Palmer, Arnold, 97
Pando, Lester, 123
Parisienne Room, 95
Park Avenue, New York, 56
Parking
  addition during 1950's, 147
  automobile space, 50
  Edgewater Club, 130
Pat-Hugo Interiors, 104
Pearl Harbor, 138
Pei, I. M., 71
Plymouth Room, 104
Political cartoons, 15
Political group founding, 12
Poray, Stanislaus Pociecha, Break, Break, Break painting, 156
Portraits
  Alexander, George L., 19
  Haskell, Charles L., 156
  Huntington, Henry Edwards, 34
  Jeffries, William Parrish, 52
  Leahy, William D., 156
  Rule, Ferd K., 19
Post, Carroll L., 129
Potter, Elmer C., 123
Potter, Newton, 113
Powell Library, 39
Pozzo, A. L., 130
Presidents
  Alexander, George L., 13, 18, 19, 23
  Austin, John, 35
  Canepa, Louis, 127, 138, 142–143
  Chamberlain, W. H., 18
  Charters, George A., 38, 44–46
  Cleary, Warren, 19
  Clemo, Bob, 19
  Cooley, John B., 123
  Edwards, LeRoy M., 122, 129, 138
  Fife, Ralph E., 62
  Houghton, Roy, 86
  Huntington, Henry Edwards. See Huntington, Henry Edwards
  Jeffries, Thomas L., 53
  Jeffries, William Parrish. See Jeffries, William Parrish
  Nerdrum, Jarl, 149
  Pozzo, A. L., 130
  Rule, Ferd K. See Rule, Ferd K.
  Smith, Dave F., 120, 122
Pritchard, Charles, 142–143
Prohibition
  gambling, 115
  hiding of bottles during police raid, 114
  opening of the Club, 85, 91
  repeal of, 113
Pumpkin Garden, 106, 107
Purpose of the Club, 169

Puthoff, Hanson Duvall
  background, 159
  East Sierra Landscape painting, 159
portrait of George Alexander, 19
Putnam, Robert, Bowling Alone book, 169

R
Ralphs, Walter W., 129
"Ramona", 48
Rationing, 139
Reading Room features, 33, 81 pictured, 20, 29
Reagan, Ronald and Nancy, 96–97, 98
Reagan Distinguished American Award, 96–97
Reagan Room, 95–96
Reception Room, 20
Red Star Men, 46, 55
Redmond, Granville
  background, 155
  California Landscape painting, 154, 155
  Marine Oil Painting, 154
Regular Life Member, 118, 120
Reiffel, Charles, Landscape painting, 162
Renaissance Room, 96
Rendler, J. C., 118, 121
Renovations in 1970, 71, 149
  Billiard Room/Tap Room, 85–89
  Edgewater Club, 130, 132, 133
  elevators, 75
  Game Room/Grill Room, 93
  Lobby, 71–74
  sports and fitness area, 107
  women's spaces, 75, 95–96
Republicans
  Jonathan Club founding, 12
  non-partisan as of 1896, 13
  voters in 1894, 10
Residential rooms
  condominiums, 150
  Edgewater Club, 129
  eighth floor, 110, 112
  eleventh floor, 110, 112
  ninth floor, 110, 112
  number of rooms, 33
  prices, 110
  seventh floor, 110, 112
  sixth floor, 110
  tenth floor, 110, 112
  twelfth floor, 110
Rickenbacker, E. V., 139
Ringe Estate, 39
Roberts, Jack D., 141
Robinson, Ray D., 38–39, 118
Roof garden, 29, 33
Roof Garden room, 115
Rossetti, W. Bunker, 118
Royce Hall, 39
Rule, Ferd K.
  background, 19, 22
  election scandal, 26
  opening of Club, 52
  portrait, 19
  presidential duties from Huntington, 35
Rule & Sons insurance firm, 46

S
Salt Lake Railroad, 19
San Gabriel Valley Water Company, 34
Santa Monica facility. See Beach Club
Santa Monica Freeway, 132
Schilling, Myron F., 51
Schultz, George, 97
Schultze, Leonard
  background, 56–57
  club architects, 45, 56–57, 110, 114
  false walls and secret spaces, 114
  impact of the Depression, 118
  new building plans, 45
  other buildings designed, 57–59
  residential rooms, 110
Scott, L. Ewing, 113
Sea Breeze Beach Club
  history, 134
  purchase, 39, 123, 127
Seafood trolley, 91
Seaver, Gertrude L., property, 118, 123
Second Mortgage Bonds, 122–123
Seventh floor, 110, 112
Sheets, Millard Owen, Fisherman's Wharf, San Francisco painting, 167
Shirey, George, 141

Siemer, Christian
  background, 157
  Huntington Library painting, 157
  View of Pasadena painting, 157
Signal light, 132
Sixth and Figueroa location. See also Town Club
  athletic club amenities, 51
  automobile parking, 50
  Bellevue Terrace Hotel, 48–49, 77
  building construction, 44–46
  club benefits, 51
  drug store, 51
  floral shop, 51
  game emporium, 51
  material suppliers, 55
  opening celebration, 50
  overnight rooms, 51, 110–113
  Schultze and Weaver, architects, 45, 56–57, 110, 114
  Solarium, 51, 114
Sixth floor, 110
Sky Bar, 115
Sky Room, 115
Slot machines, 114–115
Smeraldi, Giovanni Battista
  background, 66
  ceilings repainted, 71
  Main Dining Room ceiling, 103
  Tap Room ceiling, 85, 86, 89
  Town Club artisan, 66–67, 86, 89, 103
Smeraldi, John D. See Smeraldi, Giovanni Battista
Smith, Charles L. A.
  background, 156, 160
  portrait of Charles Haskell, 156
  Through The Sycamores painting, 160
Smith, Dave F., 120, 122
Smith, Jack Wilkinson
  background, 161
  first Artists' Life Member, 154, 156
  Marine Coastal Landscape painting, 166
  Mountain Glacier painting, 161
Smoking
  cigar counter, 70, 74
  Cigar Society, 115
  in the game emporium, 51
  prohibitions, 115
Smoking Room, 21
Social club founding and charter, 12, 14, 18
Solarium, 51, 114
South Spring Street
  move to Pacific Electric Company, 26
  next door relocation, 11, 18
  official opening, 12
  original home, 10–11
social club charter, 18
Southern California Chapter of the American Institute of Architects, 62
Southern California Telephone Company, 46
Special Committee, 119–120
Special Life Member, 118, 120
Sports and fitness
  athletic club amenities, 51, 106
  Edgewater Club, 128, 130, 132
  fifth floor, 106–109
  golfing, 106
  Pumpkin Garden, 106, 107
  renovations, 107
  running track, 107
  slot machine placement, 115
  sports bar, 86
  tennis courts, 107, 108, 130, 132
  Turkish Bath Department, 106
  Violet-Ray room, 107
Spray, Joseph, 142–143
Stag Game Room, 91
Stage comedy, 15
Stage of Pacific Electric Building, 31
Staples Center, 150
State Coastal Commission, 151
Statistics, 10, 168
Steiner, Fred A., 141
Stock, A. J., 112
Stone, Edward Durell, 56
Stories at the Pacific Electric Building
  avocado industry, 36
  Bonfilio affair, 37
  California Club police raid, 37
  Jonathan Club of Mexico, 38–39
  UCLA, 39
Street lights, 10

Sunset Boulevard, 49
Sunset North, 133
Suppliers in 1925, 55
Surf Rider, 132
Swihart, John, 97

T
Tadich Grill, 93
Tap Room, 21, 31, 85–89
Taylor, George P., 23
Tecate, Mexico, 38–39
Teidjens, Willi, Ducks in a Pond painting, 156
Telephones, 115
Television room, 115
Tenth floor, 110, 112
Thirteenth floor, 114–115
Thompson, Whiting, 79
Thrash, Ben, 128
Tiffany & Co. medallion, 96
Timelines
 1781-1894, 10–11
 1894-1903, 20
 1904-1923, 26–27
 1924-1928, 44–45
 1929-1935, 118–119
 1940-1945, 139
 1950's, 146–147
 1960's, 147–148
 1970's, 149–151
 1980's, 149–151
Todd, George Noble, 27
Top Deck, 115
Topside, 115
Town Club. See also Sixth and Figueroa location
 architecture, 56
 artisan Smeraldi, 66–67, 86, 89, 103
 barber shop, 74, 76
 Billiard Room/Tap Room, 21, 31, 85–89
 eighth floor, 110, 112
 elevator. See Elevators
 eleventh floor, 110, 112
 fifth floor, 106–109
 Florentine Lounge, 98
 fourth floor, 104–105
 front entrance, 65
 Game Room/Grill Room, 90–93
 garage, 79, 147, 149
 gift shop, 48, 77
 Grill Room, 67, 90–93
 illustrations, 60–65
 Library, 81–83
 Lobby. See Lobby, Town Club
 Main Dining Room. See Main Dining Room
 ninth floor, 110, 112
 Reagan Room, 95–96
 residential rooms. See Residential rooms
 seventh floor, 110, 112
 sixth floor, 110
 tenth floor, 110, 112
 thirteenth floor, 114–115
 twelfth floor, 110
Trains
 Jonathan Club car, 120
 Pacific Electric Building station, 32, 33
 Pacific Electric Company, 34–35
 Pacific Electric Railway, 35, 44–45
Transportation
 garage, 79, 147, 149
 parking space, 50, 130, 147
 trains. See Trains
 trolleys, 50
Triunfo Country club, 39
Trolleys, 50, 91
Truman, Harry S., 139
Trumbull, Jonathan, 17
Tufts, Edward B., 14, 17, 23
Tufts-Lyon Arms Co., 18
Turkish Bath Department, 106
Turkish room, 33
Turner, C. J., 142–143
Tuscan Terrace, 115
Twelfth floor, 110

U
UCLA, 39
Uncle Sam
 costume, 15
 named after Sam Wilson, 17
 symbol of America, 14, 15
The Unembarrassed Muse, 14

Union League Club of Los Angeles, 18
U.S. Equal Opportunity Employment Commission, 150

V
Valentino, Rudolph, 129
Verge, Gene, 134
Violet-Ray room, 107
Vorspan, Max, 150

W
The Wall Street Journal, 146
Want, Harold O., 141
War
 blackouts, 112, 139
 Edgewater Club operating hours, 130
 food stockpiling, 138
 impact on the Club, 138–139
 Key Men organization, 113
 Lusitania, 27
 Marion Flay Baugh Memorial Beacon, 140–141
 Pearl Harbor, 138
 rationing, 139
 Town Club neglect, 71
War Manpower Commission, 139
World War I, 27
Washington, George, 17
Watts, W. S., 123
Watts riots, 147
Wayland, Alice, 17
Weaver, Spencer Fullerton
 background, 56–57
 club architects, 45, 56–57, 110, 114
 false walls and secret spaces, 114
 golden spade presentation, 46
 impact of the Depression, 118
 other buildings designed, 57–59
 residential rooms, 110
Webster, H. G., 93
West Indies room, 104
Westport Beach Club, 132
White, Charles, 23
Widows, 118, 151
Wilson, Pete, 96
Wilson, Sam, 17
Women
 discrimination, 149, 150–151
 Edgewater Club sleeping rooms, 129
 elevator permanently closed, 148
 elevators, 70, 75, 95–96, 149
 Grill Room for men only, 91
 Ladies' Dining Room, 33, 95–96
 Ladies' Lounge, 95–96
 Ladies' Waiting Room, 70
 memberships, 150, 151
 at Pacific Electric Building, 95
 Reagan Room, 95
 repeal of prohibition, 113
 in residential rooms, 113
 room renovations, 75, 95–96
 separate entrance, 33, 70, 95
 Turkish Bath, 107
Waiting Room, 70
walk through the garage, 147
widows, 118, 151
Wooden, John, 97
Woolwine, Thomas Lee, 37
Wuerker, Otto, 113

Y
Yacht Club, 112
Yankee Doodle, 14
Young, Brigham, 34

Z
Zuckerman property, 118, 120, 123

Photo Credits
Jonathan Club archive collection:
 10, 11, 13 (both),14-15 (all), 16, 17, 18, 20 (all), 21 (all), 22-23 (all), 28. 29 (Bottom 31B, 32T, 37, 44, 54-55 (all), 58-59 (all), 60 (both), 61, 62 (all), 63, 65 (all), 66 (Black-and-white), 70T, 70B, 71, 73 (all), 76B, 78, 79, 80, 81 (all), 84, 86, 89t, 90, 91, 95 (Both), 96 (all), 97 (all), 98 (all), 99L, 104 (both), 106T, 106B, 107, 108, 109, 110 (all), 111, 112 (all), 113, 114 (both), 115, 119, 120, 126T, 127 (all), 128 (all), 129, 130B (both), 132 BR, 135BL, 138, 141 (all), 142, 148T
Owen Haggerty photography of Jonathan Club Art Collection and Jonathan Art Foundation collection:
 19 (both), 34, 52, 105, 139, 155-167
Douglas Hill Photography:
 12T, 12B, 50. 64, 66 (color), 67 (all), 70M, 72, 75, 77T, 82, 83 (all), 102, 103 (all), 106M, 114T, 126B, 130T, 130M, 131T, 132BL, 132 BM, 133 (all), 140 (both), 148B
Reproduced by permission of The Huntington Library, San Marino, California:
 29TL and TR, 30 (both), 31T, 34 BL and BR, 40-41, 48, 49T, 49BR, 74 (both), 76T, 77B
Los Angeles Public Library: 32B, 33 (both)
Courtesy of California Avocado Commission: 36
Courtesy UCLA: 39
The Wolfsonian – Florida International University, Miami Beach, Florida, The Mitchell Wolfson, Jr. Collection; Photo: Silvia Ros:
 56TL (Photograph by Kaiden-Keystone Studios), 56TR (Photograph by Park Lane Studios), 57
Collection of Ernest Marquez: 135T
Robert Glenn Ketchum: 166B